HOLISTIC CONS

Phiroz Mehta was born in India i… son of Parsi parents. He was educated at Royal College, Colombo, and later at Trinity College, Cambridge. Brought up in the Zarathustrian tradition, his quest for religious truth began at an early age. His study and practice of the world's great religions led him to a personal discovery of the one Way which lies at their heart. He has been described as 'at once a scholar, a mystic, an idealist and a realist', and is the author of *Early Indian Religious Thought*, *Zarathushtra – The Transcendental Vision*, *The Heart of Religion* and *Buddhahood*.

By the same author

Early Indian Religious Thought
The Heart of Religion
Zarathushtra – The Transcendental Vision
Buddhahood

HOLISTIC CONSCIOUSNESS

Reflections on the Destiny of Humanity

P. D. Mehta

Edited by
John Snelling

ELEMENT BOOKS

First published in 1989 by
Element Books Limited
Longmead, Shaftesbury, Dorset

Designed by Jenny Liddle
Cover design by Max Fairbrother
Typeset by Selectmove
Printed and bound in Great Britain by
Billings, Hylton Road, Worcester

British Library Cataloguing in Publication data
Mehta, Phiroz, 1902–
Holistic consciousness: reflections on the destiny of humanity.
1. Holistic explanation
I. Title II. Snelling, John, 1943 –
160
1SBN 1–85230–108–2

Dedicated to
SILVIA

my good and faithful wife
(born 1911, married 1939, died 1988)

In loving and reverent memory of
One who was more than a better half to me;
One who cared so deeply for all that lives.
Together we knew the laughter and tears of bliss and sorrow.
Out of the grief of her death flashes the light of love's immortality.

And with deep regard and gratitude to Four Strong Friends:
Professor Noel Q. King
John H. Moore
Valerie M. Tompkins
Victor Duret

Acknowledgements

Grateful thanks are due to Frank Andrews, Professor of General Science at the University of California, Santa Cruz, and to Tycho Silver-Photiou, for reading through Chapter 3 and suggesting alterations. Also to Carolyn Martin for word-processing the text, to Messrs Element Books for the care taken in the production of the finished book and to Michael Mann for his constant encouragement.

Special thanks are due to John Snelling for his expert editorial work and for adding paragraphs on pages 52, 53, 63 and 64 to round off the related subject matter.

Contents

Abbreviations

B.G.	Bhagavad Gita
B.U.	Brihadaranyaka Upanishad
C.U.	Chandogya Upanishad
Cor.	Corinthians
D.	Digha Nikaya
Exod.	Exodus
Gen.	Genesis
Lev.	Leviticus
Matt.	Matthew
RV.	Rigveda
Ys.	Yasna

Note on the Text

As a general rule capitalization indicates that a given word or phrase is being used in its transcendental or absolute sense.

•

I specifically use the capitalized terms 'Transcendence', 'Origin' (see p. 4 of Prologue), 'Totality', 'Atman', 'Absolute', 'Godhead' and 'God', as well as the phrases 'Primordial Undifferentiated Creative Energy' (or simply 'Primordial Creative Energy', or just 'Creative Energy'), 'One Total Reality' and 'the Infinite-Eternal' as equivalents of the Upanishadic Brahman; i.e. the Absolute All embracing both the manifest and the unmanifest, being and non-being, etc., etc. This is cognate with the Buddha's Unborn, Unbecome, Unmade, Uncompounded. . . We are not talking here about an entity but of that which is inconceivable, ungraspable, indescribable and unknowable in the ordinary sense. . .

•

Something also needs to be said about my use of those highly-charged terms, 'sin' and 'evil'. They have nowadays become encrusted with all kinds of unfortunate and erroneous connotations. In particular, they are linked with conventional notions of harsh judgement by a personal God and punishment in an eternal hell realm. I hope I make it fully clear in the course of this book that I regard such things as thoroughly nonsensical and pernicious. When I use these terms, I mean them in their old, unfallen sense of *that which spoils, obstructs or frustrates the essential unity and harmony of the Universe* – and thereby causes suffering, both to oneself, to others and to the Totality.

•

Finally, as regards non-English terminology, I have in the interests of making the work fully accessible to the general Western reader reduced the use of accents and italicization to a minimum and done away with all diacritical marks; I have however indicated the meanings of specialist terms or phrases internally in the text.

P. D. M.

Preface

This little book attempts to present, as far as lies in the writer's ability, what vision has been granted him. It is not his achievement. Truth, beauty and all that is most worthy in human life are manifestations of the grace of Transcendence. They owe nothing to any mortal's striving and endeavour, though such efforts can prepare a person to recognize and humbly acknowledge Grace when it suffuses him. Grace, it might be added, is universally present; it is not bestowed as a special favour for a particular person, nor paid as a reward for personal excellence.

The writer had no personal motive for writing this book. He simply wrote what came to him with no conceit that it might help or improve anyone. If it 'does good', so much the better; if it fails, waste no regrets on it. If, on the other hand, it annoys or bores you – and in today's world too many people indulge unnecessarily in boredom – don't blame either yourself or the writer. Earth respects the dignity of man and offers ample living room for all. May the writer be forgiven his errors.

Though it may be philosophical, this book is not just 'another philosophy' to be eventually thrown on the scrap-heap of the many philosophies that the world has already spawned.

What is it then?

If you were to ask a hundred people, 'Who or what are you?' they would answer, 'I am a doctor. . . actor, schoolmaster, shopkeeper' – or, 'An Englishman, Indian, Japanese, Russian. . .,' etc. etc. Barely ten will answer, 'I am a human being.' And of those ten, who will know the significance and implications of being human?

If what follows sheds any light on the great mystery of what it means to be truly human, the writer can die in peace.

Forest Hill, London
1988

Prologue

ONCE UPON A time there was a very young boy. Brimming over with curiosity, he pestered his mother endlessly with questions – especially, 'What is immortality?'

No clear answer ever came.

He eagerly sought elsewhere. Seriously he considered.

Still no clear answer.

Then he watched calmly and patiently . . .

Half a century passed before he began to see for himself that truth enters the person whose psyche is pure and whose mind is always open and alert. He saw then that insight could be the clarifying point of intellectual penetration into the nature of our worldly life of material and cultural strife; *or* it could be an enlightening flash of Transcendence when the psyche was pure and at peace, in harmony with itself and in right relationship with the world. In such a case there is a state of revelation, of illumined and ineffable being. No striving here, no intellectual attainment; simply, a very different mode of awareness – a transcendent consciousness, in fact.

Silently our friend continued to watch . . .

Seeing these different types of insight, he wondered for the next two decades, 'What is the nature of that transmuted consciousness which characterizes all authentic spiritual teachers?' Great world-religions based upon their teachings have become established, with immense consequences for mankind.

It must be clearly understood that the formulation of insights as concepts, however deep or inspiring, couched in language however poetic or uplifting, dims the light of the original transcendental flash in consciousness, because that vision is shapeless and formless. Truth transmutes our mode of awareness of self and of all existence. The transmuted consciousness functions as pure being and creative action. It is indescribable; but although it is beyond thought and speech, it subsumes all thought and speech, thus linking two apparently unbridgeable modes of consciousness and making it possible to emerge out of worldly mortality into immortal Transcendence whilst still living in the body.

Waiting at the edge of non-existence, you, my companion, and I, your old friend, stared into the dark. Gently, the still silence radiated a warm light suffusing sphere within sphere of empty, measureless void with love and life. Existence was born with song and dance. There-then was One Alone. And One Alone decorated the deep with the countless All. And the All was this One. And this One and the All were the None. So it was, so it is, and so it will always be with the Infinite-Eternal. This was written in the *Book of No-sayings*.

You, the reader, may say, 'This sounds like nonsense'. And how right you are from your point of view – that of common sense. I used your very words in times past. But I am old now, past immaturity and maturity, and have left both non-sense and common sense far behind. Those two contraries will continue to play games as long as vigorous young sub-humans remain sub-human; and so long as the contraries remain tangled twins – dualities – there will be love-making and make-believing, and play which becomes hate and war, and pleasure and joy which become pain and grief, and temporal living darkening into ever dying . . . until at last a grey twilight covers all and the silence is torn when the Big Bang shatters the void in a senseless frenzy.

And yet the voidness remains . . .

As for me, my limbs have lost their strength now. I move no more but stay poised in a plenum void. Knowledge has vanished too. There is only vision, non-descript and all-embracing, negating all birth and death; not proclaiming life and creation but itself *being* life and creation, the darkness of the deep and the immaculate womb of the light of the worlds, seen and unseen, known and unknown.

•

Leave the self, that source of silly sorrowing, sinking and suffering. Possessed of freedom from the self, let us together see the unseen: Origin. Not *an* origin, for that is born of ignorance and time, and is therefore doomed to die; not *the* Origin[1], for that is just a dogmatic fixation which will play havoc with you, torturing you with images of heaven and hell till you are completely bewildered; but just Origin, which will simply smile at us for having lost what is always *here-now* with us and in us. It is the All/No-thing, the One/Everything. But we must not move towards it wanting to find out what it is – remember how Psyche lost Eros. Nor must we try to run away from it, for the bark of the Heavenly Hound will transfix us to the spot. Origin *is* us, *is* all. It holds us forever, not against our will, for we have no will other than that which proceeds from Origin.

'Stop rambling on and tell me *some-thing* I can get my teeth into!' cried my companion.

'There is nothing to tell you, you who are me I who am you. That is why I am talking and will keep on talking till everything sleeps and only Origin *is*, which is the same as *I am, you are, it is.*'

'You're crazy! Go away!

'Go? You go away . . . Well, what's stopping you?'

'You seem to be holding me with some strange invisible power. Are you a kind of demon?'

'Don't you see, my dear, if you will be uncrazy, I am bound to be seen as crazy. If you will be the angel, I am necessarily the devil . . .'

And so we waited . . .

[1]But we shall say 'the origin' as and when the context or the rhythmic flow of language requires it.

Suddenly, Origin moved – or so it seemed (it is all a seeming to be so) – and there was a God Almighty BANG! We were flung out into nowhere, which is *now-here*, and ever since we have been rooted to the same spot.

Sounds crazy? But surely all of us, excepting a non-existent you, are crazy. We are all bound to be crazy if we light a candle and then rush about frantically searching for that very same candle.

Drop your candle. Stand still and be silent. Now your formerly blinded eyes will see the quenchless light of Transcendence. And you will feel fear. Such are the beginnings of wisdom . . .

Once I rushed about searching frantically. What folly that was! We can search only for something we already know at least in some slight degree. How else can we recognise it when we do meet it?

Wisdom lies hidden in me, for I, potentially, am wisdom's being, even as I am potentially the soul of truth and love and goodness and beauty. Being ignorant of the fact, I rush about frantically searching for it *outside* myself. Frantic rushing rarely avoids a disastrous collision!

Oh, the sorrow of it all!

•

All existence is sacred, for it was created by Transcendence and procreated through Nature, which is one with Transcendence. All existence is expressed as a transmogrification of the substance[1], of Transcendence, though the fact it is eliminated or pushed out of Transcendence does not imply degradation. In Nature, anything that is eliminated by one form of existence is sustenance for some other form, for interaction and interdependence are universally prevalent throughout Totality. Thus, Transcendence and existence interact with each other, though whilst the dependence of existence upon Transcendence is obvious to most of

[1]*Transmogrification*: a transformation as by magic; substance (Latin *sub-stans*), that underlying something (immaterial) which becomes matter as we experience or know it.

us, the dependence of Transcendence upon existence is sensed only by the few.

The fulfilment of the creative activity of Transcendence is made possible only by right response on the part of existence. Transcendence is order, harmony, beauty – though actually Transcendence is inexpressible, and the only true response is to observe a noble silence. Since, however, there are those with inquiring minds, people eager to explore, recourse must be made to words and concepts, and even if these are lame and inadequate, they can be useful to those who care sufficiently. The passion for truth will heal the hurtful result of mistakes; the smart of pain and the wound of sorrow will challenge, urge and drive us on along our own unique road to the supreme awakening possible for the human species.

Man and God, though existentially separate, are essentially one. Transcendence unceasingly affirms 'I am God' through every single atom of its expression, the existing Universe. This is the music of the spheres; the primordial order, harmony and beauty of the creative activity of Transcendence. So that man may realize this, Transcendence produced opposites. In truth these are not irreconcilable contraries but complementary or playfully interacting dualities. They are necessary and indispensable for man's awakening and perfection, and for his safe and blissful return to the primordial silence and peace where lies the death of the struggle between good and evil. And then death itself shines forth gloriously as the inverse face of life.

•

The life of the human race has had its peaks and troughs of civilization and barbarism, progress and regression, humanity and savagery – all seesawing through time. Perhaps it would be more correct to say that the dualities manifest together, with a tendency for one to tip the balance in its favour. When the balance favours barbarism and regression, a culture eventually suffers the pangs of death. The world today seems to be approaching such a critical point. The savagery and the frequency of crimes against both the person and the community have increased alarmingly since World War II. Affluence linked with maldistribution of wealth and resources play their part in all this. But it has all happened before. Great civilizations, like Rome, suffered moral decay and eventual destruction on the heels of affluence.

Decent austerity and self-restraint are necessary and indispensable factors for stability and freedom. The inner life is the most powerful determining factor of the outer state. Only if a person is true and pure can he be really practical: a bulwark against disaster and destruction, the founder and preserver of peace and well-being.

In the present critical global situation, it is incumbent on all of us to live as mature adults, consider the plight of the world seriously and mobilise all our strength and abilities in the service of a vision of goodness and rightness. If the children of men live truly humanly, in peace and love, they are truly the inheritors of heaven on earth.

An Ancient Indian Tale

Long ago in India a king of Sravasti ordered one of his servants to gather together all the men in the city who had been born blind. The servant did so; then the king asked him to present an elephant to them. To one group of blind men the elephant's head was presented, to another the ear – and so on till all the blind men had handled some part or other.

Then the king went up to the blind men and said, 'Well, have you handled the elephant?'

'Yes, Your Majesty,' they answered.

'Then tell me: what sort of a thing is an elephant?'

Those who had touched the head declared the elephant was like a water-pot; those who had touched the ear, like a winnowing basket; the tusk, a ploughshare; the trunk, a plough; the body, a granary; the foot, a pillar; the back, a mortar; the tail, a pestle; the tuft of the tail, a besom.

Whereupon they fell to quarrelling, shouting – *'No, an elephant is not like that!' . . . 'Yes it is!'* – till they came to blows.

In this story, different parts of the elephant were presented to the various blind men, never the whole elephant, and only the sense of touch was used for observation; so it is not surprizing that their answers were not only incorrect but also absurd. The story nevertheless makes a valid point: judgments, opinions, convictions, born of ignorance and/or based on limited or faulty observation, inevitably lead to wrangling disputations, quarrels, violence and, as history amply proves, to destructive wars.

The brain constantly receives impressions through the sense organs. Using the faculty of speech, we give names to the objects, persons, events, etc., which are the sources of these impressions. These names, which are symbolic sounds, are labels which enable us to identify the objects which they signify. According to the sense which is functioning at any given time, a person says: 'I see a tree . . .' 'I hear the door-bell . . .' 'I smell a rose . . .' 'I am touching a feather . . .' 'I taste honey . . .' In making these statements he or she is affirming that he *is conscious* of the sight of a tree, the sound of the door-bell, the perfume of the rose, the feel of the feather, the sweetness of the honey.

Attention plays an indispensable part in being conscious. If we want to know the truth about something we must observe it carefully; we must pay full attention to it. This voluntarily directed attention enables us to be clearly conscious of all the sense impressions that the brain receives from the object. 'Being conscious' means being in a state of mental alertness and receptivity; this enables us to know what we perceive and experience. It is different from being aware, for awareness is usually less sharply defined than consciousness. You can be vaguely aware, even well aware; but where consciousness is concerned you are always fully conscious; that is, really awake, perfectly attentive.

If, for instance, a man walking to his office is intensely preoccupied with a problem, he may fail to be conscious of a lamp-post next to a stationary car which has its engine running, although they stand conspicuously in his line of vision. If then he were to receive a sufficiently powerful stimulus – the backfiring of the car, perhaps, or himself bumping into the lamp-post – his attention would be forcibly detached from his problem and he would become at once fully conscious of what is actually present or happening to him.

The impressions conveyed to the brain by any or more than one sense can be confirmed, or contradicted and corrected, by other senses. In the tale of the elephant and the blind men, all the impressions produced solely by the sense of touch would have been contradicted and corrected by a sudden restoration of the sense of sight. The blind men could then have seen that the elephant was not any inanimate object but a colossal living organism. They could have seen how his ears, tusks and tail functioned; how great was the strength of his trunk and yet also how sensitive when it touched their heads ever so gently (as is done by the Thank You Elephant in Madura Temple, south India, when you have made an offering); that his speed could not match the speed of a racehorse, and so on. In short, they would have been conscious of the elephant in quite a different manner.

We take our senses for granted and tend to believe that, if we are endowed with good health and efficiently functioning sense organs, our interpretation and description of the world experienced through our five senses is the truth about the world. But is it?

Telescopes, microscopes and other modern scientific instruments have so greatly extended the field amenable to close observation that our 20th century 'truth' about the world has corrected various 'mistakes' made in the past through limited sense-based observation. We can now observe a world a millionfold greater on both the macro and the micro scales. Consequently, so much of the armchair speculation of the past has been swept away by better knowledge of the nature of things and a clearer understanding of the laws underlying material phenomena.

How reliable are our senses as instruments of perception? A blow on the head or a violent sneeze is sometimes followed by an impression of bright points of light dancing in front of the eyes. We declare, quite honestly, that we are 'seeing stars' – until we learn that the impression was caused, not by actual points of light dancing in front of us, but by the sneeze or bump causing pressure on the retina or stimulating the optic nerve to send electrical impulses which the brain interprets as flashes of light.

Again, when suffering from migraine or giddiness, we may 'see' swiftly moving patterns of light shaped like endless waves. Whilst unacquainted with the scientific explanation, we are *conscious* of such experiences only in terms of 'moving patterns of light'. But when acquainted with the scientific facts, we are, or at least can be, conscious of such experiences both as 'moving patterns of light' and also as impressions due to migraine or giddiness. Whereas being conscious of 'moving patterns of light' is directly due to sense impression, being conscious that this impression is caused by migraine or giddiness is due to acquired conceptual knowledge of the physiological mechanisms at play in the phenomenon. In other words, the inadequate manner in which we were conscious in the first instance has been modified by knowledge obtained through scientific investigation.

In the case of the blind men and the elephant, the restoration of sight would have enabled them to be conscious of the elephant as you and I are conscious, more or less.

If nature were to endow us with a sixth, unique sense organ, in what manner would we be fully conscious of our world?

Myths Ancient and Modern

CURIOSITY IS DEEPLY implanted in the human mind. Consequently, human beings have speculated through the ages about the origins of the human race and where it might be going.

Primitive man probably had only his own observations of nature and his own life-experience, plus perhaps the creative imagination, to assist his speculations. He speculated analogically: *'Just as . . . even so . . .'* His own experience showed him what lay within his power to do or control. He could kill some animals for food, destroy enemies weaker than himself, control his family and provide himself with some protection against the inclemencies of the weather, and so on. He also experienced that which was more powerful than himself: thunder and lightning, flood, tempest, volcanic eruption, earthquake and the occasional eclipse or shower of meteors. These were all great mysteries to him. The overpowering strength of the large and ferocious animals of the jungle, meanwhile, and phenomena like disease and death, were all sources of dread.

In addition to the problems posed by the forces of the environment there were psychological problems. For instance, early man must have had dreams in which he saw enemies whom he had slain, but in the dream state there was not the strength which he possessed in the waking state to overcome them, so when he woke up he must have been very perplexed and probably filled with fear. Moreover, in a dream it is usually extremely difficult to run away from whatever threatens one. How then could he deal with this situation? Was his slain enemy still existing in a mysterious form against which he could never prevail? Did he continue to exist perhaps as a disembodied spirit: a ghost, which was invulnerable? Perhaps such dreams were the source of the belief in spirits surviving after death.

There may also have been dreams of meeting dear ones who had died – parents, spouses, children, friends – happy meetings, perhaps; but such happiness seemed all too ephemeral, for soon he would wake up; moreover, it could not be repeated by merely wishing for it.

There must also have been times when early man felt dark moods of depression and fear when he imagined hostile spirits around him, or in the twilight thought he actually saw a ghastly spectre or a mob of demons dancing in laughing disarray. But he must have known contrasting moods of joyful elation when his physical prowess was at its best form and he triumphed over enemies or adverse circumstances; or when he experienced the fulfilment of his desires, most particularly in the ecstasy of love's climax with his mate.

Right from the beginning, he must also have experienced the astonishing fact that something which lay outside the scope of his knowledge at one time in his life came within it later through experience and repeated trying: that is, through unceasing experimentation. But whilst this was true in the limited sphere of physical existence, there remained that vast unknown spirit world which was much greater and altogether beyond him. Here lay perhaps the earliest stirrings of a vague awareness of Transcendence: of that which lies outside the scope of man's knowledge.

So life for early man was basically an encounter between two opposing forces: himself and his own small abilities pitted against the greater environment and the unknown and frightening world of spirits over which he had no power to deal.

Over and above these contrasting dualities, early man may have known moods of deep peace too, as when gazing at the beauty of nature he experienced a *participation mystique* and slowly slid into a semi-somnolent state of reverie, like the relaxed condition which overtakes a person just before sleep. Such a heightened experience represented the touch of Transcendence. His brain could not understand it, but in the innermost depth of consciousness there was a stir: a gentle vibration that would come to more intense life with further experience. But such moments were very rare, for in his daily life the ceaseless struggle for survival went on inexorably.

And there was this pressing question: how to deal with spirits? He could not overcome them or dominate them in any way, so he felt he must appease them. Now, just as he gave gifts as tokens of friendly submission to the strong chief of the tribe, so he offered sacrificial gifts to the spirits. And even as there was a chief of the tribe, there must be a chief of the spirits: a tribal god. Whereas visible, tangible gifts were given to the visible, tangible tribal ruler, to the invisible spirits and especially to the tribal god the gifts had to be burnt offerings and libations, for invisible spirits needed gifts which were as insubstantial as possible.

Early man invested the whole world with spirits who were endowed with extreme longevity if not actual immortality. Natural disasters were the punishment inflicted by the immortal spirits (high gods) angered by the failure of man to offer proper sacrifices or by errors in sacrificial ritual. Furthermore, just as there were male and female creatures, there were male and female spirits too; also benign and malefic gods, just as there were good and evil people.

All these beliefs and ideas as well as the rites of sacrifice grew out of analogical thinking and the imaginative speculations of ancient primitives. Out of fear and ignorance their pantheons arose. For early man had not developed sufficiently to be able to look critically at his own thought processes. He had not the means to find out the truth for himself.

Hundreds of millennia passed during which man formed strange beliefs regarding his origins: beliefs which are still today held by small groups of people in various parts of the world.[1] To cite a few examples, there are totemistic tribes who, discarding any idea of a special creation by a divine being or power, believe that their ancient ancestors sprang from animals and plants. Some Californian Indians believe that they are descended from coyotes or prairie wolves and at one time ran on all fours but, after going through many stages of development, the perfect human form was reached. One clan of the Choctaw Indians trace their descent from crayfish. The Osage Indians believe they sprang from the progeny of a pair of beavers. In East Africa, the Wanika tribe regards the hyena as its ancestor. In Malaysia some tribes believe themselves to be descended from the babacoote, a large lemur. The Bukana of New Guinea believe they derived from sea-fish, white parrots and other beasts. In Amboyna, one of the Molucca Islands, some of the indigenous people maintain that they are descended from trees. There are many similar creation myths.

Coming very close to our own day and age, we find world creation ascribed to gods or to a supreme being. There are such accounts in the Zarathushtrian scriptures, in the Book of Genesis and in Hindu writings.

In Buddhist writings there is one account ascribed to the Buddha himself (D.3.2. 28–35), though here no personal creator god is cited. In Islam, on the other hand, Allah, the One Supreme God, is the creator.

In our own 20th century we must add the creation myths of the great scientists. Various theories regarding the origin, development and nature of the universe have been propounded by such distinguished astrophysicists and mathematicians as Gamow, Lemaitre, Friedman, Planck, de Broglie, Bohm, Alpher, Herman, Omer, Fermi, Hubble, Bohr, Born, Riemann, Lobachewsky, Minkowski, Ward, Sandage, Tolman, Gold, Bondi, Hoyle, Wickramasinghe, Narliker, Chandrasekhar, Lovell, Eddington, Lyttleton, Jeans, Dirac, Burbidge, Ginzburg, Hulst, Spitzer, Whipple, Heisenberg, Hawking, Schroedinger, *et al*. There is not much concord in this little list of great names, however – and rightly so, for

See *Myths of Creation* by P. Freund, chapters 10 to 13

they are all unique individuals who needs must present unique findings. It would be true to say, though, that their scientific language is the language of present day mythology: *scientific mythology*.

All languages, whether of myth, dream, gesture or word, are merely symbolic: pictures, shadows . . . even caricatures of Reality and Truth. Nevertheless they are part of Reality: ghostly fingers pointing to Truth. When our eyes are cleansed by intelligently experienced experience, we see that Truth to which these fingers point. So also with all philosophies, religious doctrines and dogmas, and the deep states of consciousness; even holistic consciousness, though it is the apogee for us, is just the culmination of *human* consciousness and will one day become commonplace as evolution brings into being a much more developed but as yet unknown and unimaginable life form for which it will be mere maya (illusion). Revelation, Truth, Transcendence will be something quite different for the members of that coming race.

To claim that we humans represent the ultimate reach of the developmental process is proof of our lack of humility – and humiliation inexorably awaits the unhumble. All that is symbolical, all that is expressed, is maya: a passing shadow play conjured up in the sphere of mortality by Transcendence. Every shadow passes away for it is not the substance of Reality. Nevertheless it heralds the constant presence of the Immortal *Is*, the Infinite Eternal, for no shadow can ever exist without the substance of which it is the shadow.

Therefore, although holistic consciousness is postulated as the culmination of human consciousness, we must not regard it as an ultimate or as a goal for which we must strive. The ranges of Truth are endless. They had no beginning; they have no paths; they *are*, just as you the embodied Transcendence *are*. Arrive at one peak and behold innumerable other peaks; then you will know that your peak is all peaks. Such is the Infinite Eternal: no striving, no seeking – just pure being, perfect bliss.

If all seeking, striving, realizing, expressing is maya, you the reader will naturally ask: 'Why are you producing yet more maya? Why not be still and silent?'

A very proper question. Like you, I shall shut up and also shut down only after I have finished talking. Remember that Jesus said, 'It is finished'; worlds of meaning are hidden in those words. After finishing – that is, completing, doing perfectly – you shut up and shut down; for now you have, like the chrysalis which has become the butterfly, emerged out of mortality (this is the shutting down) and are the One Immortal (here is the shutting up) . . . and your silent being sings the song of truth unceasingly . . .

We strive for continuity of changeless or changing manifested existence through all time, ignorant of the fact that everlasting time is not the reality of eternity. Whilst we are here as existential beings, we *have* to produce our individual maya just as the spider spins its web out of the stuff of its own body; or like Transcendence, the Primordial Creative Energy, evolves the whole Universe out of Itself. Such is our nature. To deny it is to give rise to pain, grief, suffering. Since it is our inherent characteristic to dislike and avoid suffering, and also to help our dear ones to be free of it, we must needs express our nature in the best possible way. 'Beings follow nature. What use does repression serve?' Shri Krishna told Arjuna (B.G. 3.33).

But to say, 'It is my nature', is not, must not and cannot be used as an excuse for wrong action, for that way lies disease, destruction and death. It is only good sense to see what evil there is in my nature and to heal myself of my psychological disease. We are often told, 'You cannot change human nature', and this was true until quite recent times, if by 'human nature' we mean the genetically determined capacity of human beings. The evolutionary process effects changes extremely slowly. (Today, though, genetic engineering is a very real possibility; whether the practical application of this knowledge will prove beneficial or disastrous to mankind remains to be seen.) On the other hand, if we mean by 'human nature' the kinds of characters, temperaments, beliefs, prejudices, talents, consciences which men develop, the statement 'you cannot change human nature' is untrue since historical changes take place far more rapidly than evolutionary ones. Human beings do undergo change for better or worse throughout their lives. That great Upanishadic sage, Yājñavalkya, esteemed as the prince of yogis, affirmed: 'Truly, one becomes good by good action, bad by bad action' (B.U. 3.2.13).

Through the last six millennia or so of civilized history, men have produced their creation myths. Of these, the scientific accounts have been confined to the observable physical Universe and the evolution of the kingdoms of nature, especially of man, in whom the great stages of development are all embodied – matter, life, mind and consciousness. We tend to think of man as the crowning stage of development. This *may* be so on our planet, Earth; but may not our tendency to think this be due to inherent conceit and self-interest?

As already said, creation has been ascribed to gods or to one Supreme Being. 'God' has been the operative word. It has the great advantage of being monosyllabic, appropriate for expressing the unitary whole; but it has become heavily loaded with misconceptions. The present scientific age, in which the operative word is 'energy', calls for a different appropriate word which holds within itself the meaning of unitary wholeness.

Origin is Absolute Transcendence – Primordial Undifferentiated Creative Energy (not restricted to any of the forms of energy known to science). It is infinite, self-subsisting, self-replenishing, inexhaustible, indestructible, eternal, potentially holding within itself all that will emerge out of it. Through its ceaseless creativeness, it emanates itself as inter-related and interactive spheres within spheres of transcendent grades of being, unknowable by us, endowed with the nature of Origin, till it reaches a limited state of emanation which for us is 'The Origin', possessing the potencies of Origin. We may name three of them – creative energy, absolute consciousness (or pure mind) and fundamental substance (immaterial). These three designate the Origin for us, just as John Michael Smith – (and each name has its distinctive meaning) – identifies a single person: a unitary whole on the microscopic scale.

The Origin rests in vibrant quiescence, which in its

own transcendent context is eternal action. It is vibrant because it is alive; it is quiescent because all its potencies are in equilibrium, in unconstrained freedom, in perfect order. The equilibrium is rocked by a stir of Transcendence in eternity: a stir to become manifest, to see and know what constitutes its being. It is a stir of love, of self-love, the primal creative act, transcendental because it is devoid of any self(ish)ness. It has no cause-effect sequence, no beginning-proceeding-ending, no birth-death (for it is constantly transmutative), no form for it is infinite, and no measure or measureability. It is free blissful creativity in eternity.

In eternity there is only immediacy; no flow of time, no succession (for succession implies birth-death: a break in consciousness, a splitting up of the whole into multitudinous particulars). In the context of infinity and eternity and in the mode of consciousness maintaining in that context, there is no otherness, no separation, only simultaneity; and yet it holds countless (seemingly separate to us) particulars in a transcendent unity. To our consciousness, Transcendence is the perfectly and everlastingly paradoxical.

The vibratory creative pulse is a discontinuous, life/new-life (not a life/death) pulse. It is non-repetitive, for it constantly gives rise to a new totality. It is an incredibly swift transmutative (not transformative) renewal in eternity, not in time.

The stir of Transcendence in the Origin (our origin) releases a self-constricting activity. Creative energy differentiates and concretizes; consciousness proliferates; fundamental substance compresses into a pinpoint and bursts open explosively, producing grades of manifestation. Consciousness becomes increasingly imprisoned in the matter created by the concretization of energy and the explosion of substance. Thus our Origin changes its transcendent state of being and becomes all existence: our whole cosmos manifest in space and time. Nevertheless Transcendence remains Transcendence, not lessened by having given birth to that which in fruition before the end of time will consciously glorify and cooperate with its divine creator.

The Origin as a whole is embodied in every single one of its fragments. This is so in the context of infinity and eternity, though impossible in a purely material context. Such is the marvel of the One Total Reality. None of It is annihilated; It *all* undergoes change, which is the one changeless fact of all existence. The energy and pure mind of the Origin is the inviting power drawing imprisoned consciousness out of matter. It does not deprive or reject but rather it enlightens and sanctifies so that each fragment may awaken to its purpose as the apparatus through which Transcendence realizes its own Transcendence. This is analagous to the function of the electric light bulb in relation to electrical current.

It needs to be clearly understood that no fragments, including of course human fragments, ever achieve or attain the Transcendent. Lucifer attempted that; he rewarded himself with hell. In the stainless abode of Transcendence, achievement and attainment have no meaning, for they do not belong to unitary wholeness but to separativeness and isolativeness: to the denial of holiness, which is the basic error. Each human fragment has to live in such a manner that he or she becomes free of ignorance: of isolative selfness. Then Transcendence realizes its own transcendent fulfilment through that fragment as the perfect human, just as it is fulfilled in the perfect flower or tree or animal.

Whatsoever is manifested experiences only finite and temporal being and becoming. When it fulfils the purpose of its existence, it is transmuted into the Transcendent. Its separate existence as a manifested entity then completely disappears. The Origin alone *Is*.

So, there is nothing whatsoever for me, the particular fragment, to gain. When I have become fully *conscious* of what starts as an intellectual perception of this fact, the utmost purity – selflessness – shines divinely.

As stated already, words are merely the shadow of truth. Although the shadow heralds the presence of the Substance, the task of the existential being, myself, is to flower out into the Substance. If I am the light, I cast no shadow; but if I so live that I continue to produce shadows, which are illusions, maya, then I am not living rightly. Adam sinned by eating the fruit of the Tree of Good and Evil, for he, the psycho-physical existential being, was still imperfect and therefore not fit to eat of the Tree of Life which also stands, like the Tree of Good and Evil, in the middle of the Garden of Eden. That garden is your own psycho-physical being. No man dare drink of the wine, the Ichor, of Life Eternal, until he is at-oned with God, the Origin. Adam's sin confined and fixed his consciousness in duality, which afterwards afflicted both himself and his descendants: mankind. The thorns and thistles of confusion and conflict, sorrow and suffering, decay and death beset and darkened consciousness, not only your or my consciousness but all consciousness right up to Origin, for anything whatsoever, whether infinitesimal or cosmic, wholly affects the One Total Reality.

But just as Adam (who is myself, yourself) *had* to sin in order that the sufferings of the spirit would ultimately open the inner eye to Truth and find redemption through some other Son of God (who is yourself, myself, who is now self-sacrificing love and obedience to the law, the voice of the Divine), even so I *have* to sin by writing and speaking – only my fond conceit! – about Truth. If I only dare – and dare unto death – to do so, then I might *be* Truth Itself. So bear with me, you who are my companion for ever, for should *I* be the Light of Eternity *you* shall have the *whole* fruit of that enlightenment. Labour belongs to the mortal sphere of measurement and apportionment, but the spirit belongs to wholeness; so whatever is mine is also entirely yours.

Abstract fullness from fullness in the Infinite-Eternal and fullness remains. Therefore the hunger and thirst of myriads can be satisfied with one loaf and one cup of wine.

The Very, Very Long, in Short

THE HUMAN CHILD announces its birth with a cry. The cosmos announced its birth with a Big Bang – and immediately began to expand at an accelerating pace. Fortunately, there was no air for sound waves to spread, nor living creatures whose ear-drums could be split. *We* never heard the Big Bang nor did we see the birth. Had we been present then, this could never be written now.

Modern scientists say that the birth of this baby, the Universe, took place somewhere between 15 and 20 billion years ago. (The billion has dwindled to 1000 millions from its original million millions, but we shall oblige by using the present fashion in numeration.) Its birth certificate is written in mathematical language. It had neither parents nor midwife; it seemed to be self-conceived – you and I are the conceivers of all this – and self-born. A remarkable baby!

But why such a cosmic bang at birth? Announcement of almightiness?

Baby Cosmos was indeed remarkable. It actually started as an invisible thing – a ball of radius no more than one-thousandth of a centimetre. It was rather dense, however; some 10^{90} kilograms per cubic centimetre. And somewhat hot, 10^{31} degrees Kelvin (this scale starts at -273 degrees Celsius).

Was the birth an easy one?

Masterminds of the Big Bang Theory say that at the 'Singularity' (that is at Big Bang time, which is the beginning of all time), density being so high, gravitational stresses were capable of tearing apart the vacuum (whatever that may mean). Space-time was consequently disrupted by gravitational forces. Out of the void burst forth fullness!

At what time was this baby born?

My mathematical clock, meticulously accurate, chimed: 'At Planck Time: 10^{-43} of the first second after the Singularity.'

What was Baby Cosmos like to look at?

Beautiful! Just like your very own baby.

How shapely was it?

Wonderful! It was an immense but most unusual cloud. What it was made of I cannot say, though I recall hearing whispers, such as:

Within 10^{-43} second of the Singularity, the Big Bang created subatomic elementary particles and anti-particles. The heavier ones, such as the protons, antiprotons, neutrons, mesons, etc., are called *hadrons*. Mesons exist for hardly a millionth of a second inside the nuclei of atoms, but they help to hold each nucleus together, so even the littlest thing can exert a stabilizing influence. The lighter ones, such as the electrons, positrons, muons, etc., are called *leptons*. And there are neutrinos, massless (?) particles which move with the speed of light through anything and everything. As you read these words millions of neutrinos have moved through both you and the Earth.

Since particles and antiparticles are oppositely charged – duality existed from the beginning of the material Universe – there was terrible carnage in the very first second. For instance, annihilation took place with the merging of a positively charged positron with a negatively charged electron, a relatively large amount of energy being liberated and two photons being produced. (A photon is a quantum of electromagnetic energy.) Photons constitute the highly penetrating gamma rays. They are pure energy and have no mass.

The annihilation of particle-antiparticle pairs took place instantaneously; but the annihilation was not total – there was a residue which became the Universe in which we live. During its first few moments, the early Universe was uniformly filled with radiation and neutrinos together with electrons, protons and neutrons in relatively small quantities. It cooled rapidly as it expanded. When it was a million-year-old infant, the temperature had dropped sufficiently to enable protons and electrons to form hydrogen atoms, each consisting of one proton and one electron – the lighest known chemical element. Neutrons played an important part in synthesizing heavier elements from lighter ones (by the process of nucleosynthesis). At first the neutrons were too hot. After the first minute, the temperature had dropped to a billion degrees or so Kelvin. The neutrons then seized protons to make nuclei of deuterium, which is heavy hydrogen. Deuterium has a high absorptivity for neutrons. So, seizing another neutron, tritium was formed, which, reacting with protons, made helium. Each helium nucleus has two protons and two neutrons. There was abundant helium, less abundant deuterium (an isotope of hydrogen) and certain isotopes of lithium and boron produced in the Big Bang. These, and subatomic particles and dust-gas and dust, as it is called – constituted the original cloud which was beautiful Baby Cosmos.

Dust? you ask.

If you turn off the electrical charges on *all the atoms* of the Universe, everything would crumble down to an invisible fine dust. Without electrical forces there would not be a single 'thing' – only diffuse clouds of electrons, protons and neutrons, plus gravitating spheres of subatomic particles.

How did Baby Cosmos grow into the Universe as we see it?

This cloud of gas and dust was not entirely homogeneous (uniform). Inhomogeneities mean that there were fluctuations in the density of the cloud here and there. A very small non-uniformity at the beginning led to large condensations of matter. The density fluctuation exerted a gravitative pull on surrounding parts of the cloud. Matter became increasingly compact as it formed a galaxy, and spun faster and faster as the gravitational collapse (i.e. the compacting of matter by the gravitational pull) continued, like a die-skater bringing his arms in.

Within new-born galaxies, all the stars and solar systems are born through the gravitational collapse of interstellar gas and dust. Our universe of galaxies –

maybe a hundred billion of them – displays both order and disorder: duality again. When galaxies collide, the result is quite unlike what happens when you or I collide head on in our cars. The stars in each galaxy are so widely separated – trillions of miles away from each other – that it would usually look like a celestial ballet rather than a tragic disaster. Whilst the star-studded heavens display a wonderful beauty and obedience to law and order, they also manifest a terrible violence, chaotic and destructive in unimaginable measure, as in a quasar explosion: duality once more.

Galaxies began forming about a billion years after the birth of the cosmos. Our own galaxy, the Milky Way, started to form about 16 billion years ago. Our own solar system is about 4.5 to 5 billion years old. Although Earth is 4.6 billion years old, we know nothing of the first billion years before its crust consolidated. The oldest rocks formed a little under 4 billion years ago. Major disturbances of the crust produced changes in geography and climate, which affected the evolution of terrestrial life. This story is written in the record of the rocks.

Geologists tell us about the four eras of geological history, each of which is subdivided into systems or periods, which are sometimes again further subdivided into upper and lower: the Pre-Cambrian (or Proterozoic, First Life); the Palaeozoic (or Ancient Life, covering the periods from the Cambrian to the Permian, spanning about 375 million years); the Mesozoic (or Middle Life, covering the Triassic, Jurassic and Cretaceous Periods, spanning about 155 million years); and the Cainozoic (or Modern Life, covering the Paleocene to the present Holocene Periods, starting about 70 million years ago). From the Cambrian system to the present day covers about 600 million years.

When Earth was first formed out of its parent interstellar gas, its surface presented a barren landscape of mountains, deserts, volcanos and lava. As the hot planet cooled, water vapour condensed and seas and rivers formed. Life originated in the warm seas. How it did so at that time is a mystery, but modern laboratory experiments give us a hint. If you spark a mixture of hydrogen, methane, ammonia, hydrogen sulphide and water vapour for some minutes, you see a brownish pigment streaking down the sides of the containing vessel. The interior gets covered with a thick brown 'tar', which is a very rich collection of complex organic molecules, including the constituent parts of proteins and nucleic acids. The gases mentioned above were present in the early Earth's atmosphere, and the sparking agent was lightning. But whereas nature completed the whole process in the course of many aeons, in the laboratory, although the essential molecular building blocks can be produced, they have yet to be put together in the correct sequence. We are therefore still a long way from seeing a living creature crawl out of a test tube. There is yet much to be discovered about the origin of life, including the origin of the genetic code.

In the Pre-Cambrian Period, between about 4.5 billion and 600 million years ago, microscopic blue-green algae were the dominant life-forms filling the seas. There was no life on the land. Life was confined to the sea in the succeeding Cambrian and Ordovician Periods. After the very long dominance of the algae, a very great proliferation of life-forms took place with the advent of the Cambrian Period some 600 million years ago. There emerged worms, jellyfish, sponges and starfish; also trilobites, the most advanced creatures of that period but all extinct now, which lived on seaweeds.

In the Ordovician Period, mountain building went on in Wales and in parts of America and North West Europe. The first vertebrates appeared and in the Silurian Period new species of vertebrates developed in the sea: sea-scorpions, heavily armoured creatures nine feet long. Plant life became more varied in structure. Coral reefs developed on a large scale. The first plants developed on land, but were leafless. The Cambrian, Ordovician and Silurian Periods belong to the Lower Palaeozoic Era; the next three to the Upper Palaeozoic.

The Devonian, a period of extensive mountain building and volcanic activity, saw Earth wearing her mantle of green as plants with roots, stems and leaves evolved. These ranged from small herb-like growths to trees over 40 feet high. In the sea there was a rapid evolution of the ancestors of all modern fish – it was the 'Age of the Fish' (the fish is one of our earliest ancestors) – and the first amphibians made their appearance; also primitive sharks, about 20 feet long. With plants to feed on, the first invertebrates left the sea and adapted themselves to living on land. They included millipedes, mites, spiders and wingless insects. Certain species of insects developed wings in the Carboniferous Period, when plant and animal marine life was abundant, and giant evergreen trees over 100 feet high flourished in tropical swamps of the extremely dry period in which the coal measures were laid, especially in the Northern Hemisphere. Partly rotted vegetation accumulated as peat and then turned into coal.

In the Permian Period, land creatures, mainly the reptiles, increased in number and variety, as did insects, thus bringing the dominance by marine creatures to an end. Mountain building, glaciation and oceanic transgression (the spread of the seas over land areas) featured in this as in other eras. The development of seasonal differences in climate and temperature in the Permian Period caused evergreens to decrease in number, but deciduous plants able to withstand frost and drought made an appearance.

Next came the Mesozoic Era, lasting about 155 million years. In the Triassic Periods, early arid conditions in the Northern Hemisphere were unfavourable to plant life, but later on wetter conditions promoted the growth of cycads, ferns and conifers. In the sea, the first ichthyosaurs, carnivorous fish-shaped reptiles, flying fish and lobster-like creatures evolved, whilst reptiles dominated life on land. The first warm-blooded mammals evolved from the reptiles. The first flies and termites, and 6-inch long dinosaurs were present. Reptiles increased in size and variety in the Jurassic Period. Diplodocus was about 84 feet long and weighed about 35 tons. Such huge reptiles, too large for survival on land, lived in swamps and marshes. In the seas, meanwhile, the largest plesiosaurs were about 16 feet long. There were flying reptiles pterosaurs, having a 20-foot wing span. The first bird, archaeopterix, evolved feathers from scales, but retained reptilian teeth, solid bones and a long, feathered, vertebrate tail. Strange to think that our own sweet song-birds evolved out of slithery reptiles!

In the Cretaceous Period, giant reptiles, dinosaurs and pterosaurs dominated land and air, ichthyosaurs the sea. But towards the end of this period, about 65 million years ago, the dinosaurs, together with a great many other species of the Earth, were wiped out of existence in one catastrophic event. We are still uncertain how and why it happened. It may be that the extinction of the reptiles cleared the way for the development of mammals and humans. Tree shrews and mammals survived. The latter remained inconspicuous till the end of the period, when placental mammals, in whom the young are nourished by the mother's blood before birth, developed. In the sea, marine life continued to be dominated by reptiles, giant turtles and mosbsaurs: creatures resembling sea-serpents. Fish evolving in the period were closely related to the herrings, rays and sharks of today.

In the Miocene-Pleistocene Period, coastal land areas consisting of far-reaching swamps and slow-flowing rivers formed enormous deltas. This was also a great mountain building period: the Rockies and Andes, the Himalayas and the European mountains were all thrust up then. The Panama Ridge also emerged, giving rise to the Gulf Stream. A mild climate with alternating seasons promoted the growth of deciduous trees: fig, magnolia, poplar, plane – and the parallel evolution of insects and nectar-bearing flowers encouraged the spread of flowering plants.

The Cainozoic Era opened with the Paleocene Period starting about 70 million years ago. Tropical conditions were so widespread that tropical jungles and palms flourished in the south of England! There was moreover considerable volcanic activity. Flowering plants and deciduous trees became dominant too. The ancestors of modern mammals – the elephant, horse, rhinoceros, pig and cattle – appeared and although giant reptiles had by now disappeared, crocodiles, turtles and land tortoises evolved, as did all the insects known today. In Burma there were primitive monkeys and gibbons. In the sea, marine reptiles became extinct. Two groups of mammals, sea-cows and early whales, adapted themselves to life in the sea. Most species of fish known today appeared.

In the succeeding Oligocene Period new species of

crabs, mussels and snails evolved, whilst on land the ancestors of modern cats, dogs and bears did so too. Herbivores increased; small elephants with short trunks and tusks in both jaws, hoofed animals and giant rhinoceroses appeared. There was also a tail-less primitive ape, possibly related to the ancestors of man. Some parts of the world now had a cooler climate. Forests dwindled; grasslands and grass-eating mammals spread. The sea area diminished and the land mass grew. In Europe, the Alps began to form with extensive crustal movements.

In the next period, the Miocene, there were more extensive changes of the land mass and the Mediterranean became practically land-locked. Now Europe and Asia finally joined up to form a single Eurasian continent; the join at the Ural Mountains is much older, however. The Alps and the Himalayas meanwhile grew to their present stature. The lordly, snow-clad peaks of the Himalayas – more than a hundred of them over 24,000 feet – now look down on the rest of the world. Two comparable peaks are to be found in China; next comes Aconcaga (23,000 feet) in South America. The mild, damp climate of the period generally favoured the growth of maple, poplar, oak and, on higher ground, cedar and sequoia, whilst extensive prairies covered the North American Plains. Fish increased in variety. There was an abundance of enormous sharks, over 60 feet long and possessed of 6-inch long teeth (these and also other outsize creatures became extinct in the next period). Elephants increased in size and migrated from Africa into Europe, Asia and North America. Primitive penguins, some as tall as humans, meanwhile kept cool in Antarctica.

In the Pliocene Period, beginning about 11 million years ago, the Earth began to look something like it does today. Marine life was much as it is now. On land, many species of mammal perished. Of those that survived, one species continued to develop: you and I are the descendents, perhaps to the 300,000th generation, of those ancient venerable ancestors.

The next period, the Pleistocene, which enjoyed a lifespan of a mere 1.8 million years, was afflicted with unusually extreme climatic changes and glaciation periods, such as

Würm 1 and 2, Riss, Mindel, Gunz, going back in time in that order. As the ice melted the sea bed would rise and so would the land mass which had been pressed down by the weight of the ice. Scandinavia still rises one centimeter per year.

In this way Creative Energy prepared this beautiful Earth as a home for its long-awaited child, man, who would be fated to be exposed to the stormy winds of existence. Such has indeed been the fate of all manifestation right from the beginning, when out of the creative, crashing chaos of the Big Bang emerged the first-born of the thunder of the gods, hydrogen, accompanied by countless hosts of particles and anti-particles: the gods and demons, the devas and asuras (titans) of religious imagination.

Man, a unique creature in the whole animal kingdom, belongs to the order of primates, as classified by Linnaeus, along with the apes, monkeys and prosimians (such as lemurs). The superfamily *Hominoidea* within that order includes only the apes and humans and their extinct relatives who were nearer man than ape. Man evolved, as far as the organism is concerned, out of the primates.

It is now thought that the process started long ago in Oligocene times. Two branches stem from the higher primates of about 45 million years ago: the *Platyrrhini* or New World monkeys, who played no part in hominoid evolution, and the *Catarrhini* or Old World monkeys, classed as *Cercopithecoids* (slender-bodied long-tailed monkeys) and *Hominidae*, the group from which we hominids sprang.

Proconsul africanus, a primate the size of a baboon and the best known of the early Miocene apes, is perhaps similar to the ancestor of all apes and humans. He migrated to Asia and Europe. Fossils of *Ramapithecus* and *Sivapithecus* found in the Sivalik Himalayan region of India and Pakistan mark steps on the way to man. These are long steps, each lasting millions of years. The first definite hominids appear in Tanzania and Ethiopia. Mary Leakey and her colleagues at Laetoli in Tanzania, who uncovered the footprint evidence of hominids that walked on two legs, dated them definitely at 3.75 million years. Other evidence comes from the half-complete skeleton named 'Lucy' and specimens of *Australopithecus africanus* found by Donald Johanson and his colleagues at Hadar in Ethiopia and dated between 4 and 3 million years.

Bipedalism was an important advance in the evolution of the human organism, for it meant living on the ground and the adoption of an erect posture. *Homo erectus* struts onto the stage about 1½ million years ago. His erect posture allowed him to carry his head on the vertebral column, and the *foramen magnum* (an aperture through which the cranial cavity communicates with the vertebral canal) was shifted to the human position. Carrying the head instead of letting it hang as in the case of four-footed creatures freed some of the neck muscles, which, with correlated changes in the neck, affected the larynx, making speech possible.

Several other changes also took place affecting the eye, ear and hand. Anthropoids have forward-looking eyes; man has stereoscopic vision. The ability to distinguish sounds and register them in the brain increased in delicacy. These characteristics are linked with the growth of the frontal brain. Related to this is the development of the hand (especially the right) and the extraordinarily opposable thumb (great pianists are particularly gifted in this respect), making the hand a versatile, delicate and at times a subtly expressive organ of communication.

In the ancestral hominoids, the apes, the period of gestation is about 220 days or less. In man it is 280 days. This longer period delays hardening of the skull and increases the growth of the brain, thereby facilitating more sensitive registration of vision and hearing. All this has been intensified by the baby's much longer period of dependence after birth upon the mother.

Homo erectus was the first widely distributed hominid species, originally appearing in Africa. He was present in south-east and east Asia until about 300,000 years ago. A life-span of over a million years speaks well for the stability of his form. He probably made use of fire about 700,000 years ago. Later on, in the middle Pleistocene, archaic *Homo sapiens* (not much different from *Homo erectus*) appeared. Later still, about 45,000 years ago came anatomically modern *Homo sapiens,* definitely different from archaic *Homo sapiens* both cranially and subcranially. His stone and bone tools were more abundant than those of his predecessors. At the same time true oxen, elephants and horses appeared, though it is only during the last 10,000 years that man has learned to tame and domesticate animals and to cultivate plants.

It is essential to keep an open mind with regard to all the knowledge that we acquire. As the decades and centuries pass, advanced research and superior techniques bring new facts to light. The new is sometimes startlingly different from the old, even contradicting it and going flatly against our commonsense view of the nature of things. An outstanding example of this is the eclipse of the old mechanistic world-view established by Descartes (1596–1650) and Newton (1642–1727) by that revealed through modern Quantum Mechanics and Field Theory.

Newtonian mathematics and science, both theoretical and applied, works well enough on the macroscopic scale and within the frame of reference which sees atoms as the ultimate building blocks of all matter. The whole universe is conceived as a wonderful machine working in undeviating obedience to fixed laws. Consequently, the scientist may, in theory at any rate, exactly predict future events given adequate pre-knowledge of the forces at play and the ways in which they function. Nature is rational – apart from the occasional aberration, like an earthquake or volcanic eruption. And the atom is the rock upon which we could safely build the house of our material knowledge and certainty. We even went so far in our proud conceit as to assert our 'conquest' of Nature. True enough, this Rock of Ages, the fundamental 'stuff' of matter, was invisible and intangible – but that was simply due to its extremely small size.

Sadly, this basic particle, once as indestructible as God, went the way of all flesh – and indeed of all atoms – from the beginning of our century. Thomson, Rutherford, Chadwick, Aston and other great scientists were responsible for what we might call the Atom-Bang, as though it were the miniature of the cosmic Big Bang. As the century advanced there progressively appeared protons, electrons, neutrons, mesons and all the other '-ons' of the burgeoning sub-atomic family.

In 1900, Max Planck discovered that excited atomic oscillators emit and absorb energy only in specific amounts, not smoothly and continuously. The energy is radiated in spurts, in 'quanta'. Planck was the father of Quantum Mechanics. He also discovered a constant (h), afterwards called Planck's Constant, which never changes. It is a number which is used to calculate the size of the energy packets, the quanta. Einstein, Bohr, De Broglie, Born, Dirac, Pauli, Bohm, Heisenberg, Schroedinger, Yukawa, von Neumann – these are a few of the great names of a galaxy of physicists and mathematicians responsible for Relativity Theory, Quantum Mechanics, Quantum Field Theory, etc., which have together given rise to our century's world-view.

And what a world view it is. The search for the 'ultimate' building blocks of the universe of matter has led to the discovery that there are no such blocks. Subatomic 'particles' are immaterial; they have no objective existence. Scientists call them 'tendencies to exist' and say that they are really interactions between fields. The word 'particles' is used purely for convenience when talking about them. The early physicists saw in the photographs of thousands of bubble chamber experiments that, when they made two elementary particles collide, not only were they destroyed at the point of contact but new particles were created, as elementary as the colliding ones and often just as massive. A Shiva's Dance of Creation, a phantasm of nothing-something-nothing-something . . . or, if you like, creation-annihilation-transformation within a framework of probability and the laws of conservation.

Subatomic particles are actually pure energy; the 'material' universe is in fact pure energy. The interaction of fields mentioned above is instantaneous and at a single point in space and time, not as whole fields or gradually. The particles appear and disappear in a flash.

Whereas we think in the ordinary way that something is this *or* that, the modern view is that it can be this *and* that. Light, for example can be wave-like; it can also be particle-like, according to the experimental conditions and our approach to it. One astounding discovery in connection with experimental work in the subatomic sphere has been that the conscious observer of the experiment influences the result of the experiment. This is quite contrary to the old conviction that the person conducting the experiment was totally detached and exerted no influence whatsoever on the course or result of the experiment.

Newtonian Physics gave us laws which worked, do work and will continue to work in the macroscopic world of everyday life. So we experienced and continue to experience a sense of certainty, reliability and comfort that we live in a well-regulated Universe. Being constructed as we are, psycho-physically, with a brain and sense organs functioning as they do, we have been *conscious* of the world in the way that we are conscious (i.e. as a well-regulated material world) through very many centuries. Modern science, however, shows us that Nature is fundamentally irrational, governed by probability, subject to chance. This calls for the development of an entirely new mode of consciousness that can deal more adequately with the new world-view that is emerging.

Despite all the findings of modern science, shake the branches of an apple tree when you feel like it and delicious but indubitably *material* apples will rain down on your head. You can be rest assured of that fact.

But equally true is the fact that every single apple will be composed of countless insubstantial subatomic particles!

Self-conscious Man

DIFFERENT DEGREES OF mind and consciousness are manifested in the animal world; no clear lower limit to mind is apparent. Free, spontaneously-moving, single-celled animals such as amoeba and paramecium, besides displaying self-motivation can secure food and multiply. They have no nerves and seem devoid of sense organs, yet they exhibit preferential choice when they ingest one particular particle rather than another. The members of the coelenterata family, which includes jellyfish, sea anemones and coral, are able to delay their responses to stimuli; some scientists think that these creatures can learn. Cartilaginous fish can certainly learn.

Even the primitive capacity to learn and the exercise of preferential choice indicate the presence of mind. When we come to more evolved animal species, however, there is clear evidence of mind. A chimpanzee, for example, can be a clever toolmaker, designer and user. Untaught, he can use a crooked stick to bring down the fruit of his choice. If it is too short, he can, again without human instruction, join another stick to the first and obtain his food. Again, the horse, elephant and other animals can learn many techniques and tricks. A dog can know if an intruder is undesirable, be he a burglar or a strange animal.

In man, the play of mind comes into its own. Man's first concern was self-preservation and survival. Through hundreds of centuries he discovered ways and means to improve and control his environment and to ensure his personal safety against various inimical forces, human, animal and natural, till at last he reached the stage during the last few thousand years when he began organizing society and laying down systems of law, building cities and inventing machines. Attempting to satisfy his curiosity regarding the workings of Nature, his own being and the origin and end of all things, he produced mathematics and science, psychology and philosophy, the arts and religion. Mind was the predominant factor in all this developmental process.

Whilst mind is active in rudimentary forms in the non-human world, the human mind differs considerably from mind in all other species. We can contemplate ourselves: our birth, growth, experience, behaviour, nature, environment, the purpose(s) of our existence, our death and whether there is or is not an after-death state. We can contemplate whether life has or has not any meaning for us and/or the world; whether there is or is not that which is transcendent to us, realizable or utterly beyond us. We can contemplate whether there is or is not a relationship between ourselves and that Transcendence. If there is one, what is its nature? What does it entail in respect of the kind of life we should lead, not only in relation to Transcendence but also in relation to our fellow human beings, to the world and to all creation?

Non-human species cannot do all this, nor can they reason as we do. Animals live in accordance with the laws of their own being, in tune with Nature inasmuch as she relates to them. The hungry lioness who pounces on me in order to feed her lazy husband, cubs and herself is truly observant of the 'ethic' laid down for her by Nature. It is only good sense on my part to place the correct distance between such a queen of the jungle and an intrusive human like myself.

Between man and man there are great differences as regards mind-development and consciousness. There is man the predator, murderer, rapist, robber, destroyer. There is man the simpleton, the fool, dim-witted and unskilled. There is man the artist, scientist, philosopher, altruist, universal benefactor. And there is man the saint, the embodiment of perfect truth and love, goodness and wisdom, purity and beauty. This last man is true man – *hu-man* – the man in whom the culmination of the aeons-long human evolutionary process comes to full fruition.

Throughout a vast time-span evolution has been preparing the living body as the instrument or vehicle for man's fruition. We must appreciate the importance of the *living* body. A dead body may have some uses: in medical studies, perhaps, or forensically. But only a living human being can awaken, develop intelligence and grow in virtue – specially distinctive of *homo sapiens*. The different grades of intelligence and character seen in human beings mark the stages on the way to the fully-fledged human.

We, the innumerable multitude, can reasonably be regarded as subhuman, the prefix 'sub' simply meaning 'not yet perfectly developed'. If I, the ordinary worldly man, am still subhuman, I can and do make mistakes. We have a saying *Humanum est errare*: 'It is human to err.' This is an inadequate and misleading statement: the fact is that it is *subhuman* to err.

Let us consider the word *hu-man*. In Sanskrit we have these words: *sumanas*, meaning 'good hearted', 'good minded' (*manas* means 'mind') and *sugata* meaning 'having fared well,' 'having attained the goal happily'. *Sugata* is also a Pali word having the same meaning as the Sanskrit one. It is often applied to Gautama the Buddha, who was the master of compassion and wisdom. In the Avestan language of very ancient Iran, the *su* of Sanskrit becomes *hu*. Zarathushtra presents more succinctly the ethic of righteous living in his triple formula of *humata*, 'good thought', *hukhta*, 'good word' and *hvarshta*, 'good deed'. The prefix *hu* in *hu-man* may well stand for good in the supreme sense – the goal of perfect truth happily or blissfully attained.

What of the *man* part in human? The Sanskrit dictionary says that the root *man* means 'to think'. That is a very poor meaning, for what we in our ordinary state call 'thinking' is merely silent talking, inaudible chatter, usually if not entirely self-centred. Transcendence never chatters. We can discern a true and worthy meaning, however, if we look into one of the Trismegistic teachings: the discourse to Hermes Trismegistus by the Divine Pymander (Ποιμανδρησ) shepherd and teacher of men and the ideal archetype of all mankind.

He says: 'I am Pymander. I am the Light, the pure Mind (νουσ). The Word of Light from nous is the Creative Word, the Logos, the Son of God'.

This Creative Word is called 'the thought in the mind of God', which is not a stream of words but the creative energy of pure mind (of God). If we can truly see this through the right activity of nous (νουσ): 'unerring insight', (buddhi or prajña in Sanskrit), we begin to sense the transcendent root of what we mortals call *thought* and *thinking*, and to understand very subtly the deep meaning of the root *man*. We may well say it is *creative action in eternity*, or Transcendence thinking the thought which is archetypal man. We must note that in the Trismegistic teachings God is called *All-Father Mind*. How close is this to the citta matra or 'mind only' teaching of the Mahayana Buddhist Yogacara school that pure mind is the origin of everything?

The thought in the divine mind is transcendent creative energy. The 'thinking-speaking' by Transcendence is pure revelation: wordless, not conveyed or perceived as idea or thought in our ordinary meaning of those words but as immediate, direct, shapeless and formless realization in and by holistic consciousness. This has profound effect upon the psycho-physical organism, purifying and energizing it, even transfiguring it. Later on the brain may be able to give it shape and form as inspired idea and word, which indeed is prophetic speech. Revelation's context is the infinite-eternal, the immortal. Space-time is the context of concept and word, the mortal, the finite and temporal.

The fully-fledged human can be clearly conscious of this and know for certain that the profound meaning of *hu-man* is 'blissful creator'. A fleeting taste of this blissful creativeness is experienced, practically unknowingly, in the ecstasy of biological creation – creation, not mere sensational excitement. It is experienced more intensely in cultural creation flowing from profound insight or the inspiration of genius. Most completely as far as is possible for one in the human state, it is experienced in the ecstacy of mystical unity in Transcendence.

In cultural creation, which is actually a *procreation* in art, science or philosophy, etc., a psychical analogue of biological procreation, you are still conscious that you, the separate individual, are a little god. In mystical unification, the isolated 'you' has vanished. After emerging out of that transcendent state you know that Transcendence has realized its own transcendent being through 'you', the perfected one, the fully-fledged human. Not unto 'me' the glory, for 'I' am mortal. Death is lord over 'me'. 'My' task is to allow right self-purification to come about so that I see the vision and afterwards live as the spontaneous co-operator with the evolutionary process till the end of my days.

•

Over five billion members of the species *homo sapiens* populate the world today. Of these, fully-fledged humans are an extreme rarity. There is, however, a numerable group on the way to fruition as well as the innumerable multitude of ordinary subhumans. And there is the perhaps not so small group of devilish individuals scattered over the globe.

In what manner am I, the ordinary subhuman, conscious of myself and of the world?

During infancy I become aware of myself as the body and the needs of the body: an indentification which persists throughout life. Whatever is outside my skin is *not-me*. Bits of it may be mine – my mummy or daddy, my teddy bear or doll – but collectively it is all not-self. This consciousness of self and not-self intensifies throughout childhood and accordingly possessiveness becomes stronger and stronger. This separation of self and not-self is rooted in and maintained by the functioning of our sense organs. There is a distance between what is sensed and the subject who senses. This native isolativeness and separativeness is the root source of all our conflicts and disharmonies throughout life.

During childhood and adolescence I associate my feelings, thoughts, desires, perceptions, knowledge, qualities, abilities and skills (both physical and mental) with my self. The psycho-physical organism and all its activities constitute the 'me': a 'me' that is different and separate from every other 'me' in the world. In conversation or any other mode of communication, this 'me' is referred to as 'I', every other person as 'you', 'he' or 'she'. If I have had a conventionally religious upbringing and education, I may believe, even though I do not see and know for myself, that a super-being named God, the creator of everything, has endowed me with bodily life and a spirit or soul, which is of the essence of God and, like God, immortal. At this stage of my growth, immortality simply means living as a spirit for ever and ever (an indefinitely extended temporality) as an identifiable entity, in the wonderfully happy place or state known as 'heaven' if I have lived a religiously good life, or in its inverse, 'hell', if I have lived an evil life.

So 'I' am an immortal spirit residing in a temporal body and endowed with a mind. Such is my self-consciousness of myself, and I assume that everyone else in the world is self-conscious in much the same way. Unbiased close observation shows that the innumerable multitude is in fact isolatively and separatively self-conscious, even though many of us may love family members and/or friends very deeply indeed. Only holistic consciousness is free of any sense of separateness or otherness with respect to that which we have called the not-self.

The self-consciousness of each and every member of the human race is different from that of every other member. Each psycho-physical organism is unique because no two persons are exactly alike in every respect. Nature's variety is as inexhaustible as that of the creative activity of Transcendence.

Consider briefly the procreative process. Each parent produces a mature reproductive cell called a gamete. The development of a male or female gamete differs from that of a non-reproductive cell, for it involves *the rearrangement of the genetic material inherited by each parent from their parents*. The union of the male and female gametes produces a zygote, which develops into a new individual that is different from the parents and from any person that ever was, is now or will be. He or she is a *new* creature with *new* possibilities of mental and spiritual development, dependent upon environmental influences, the organism's development and the innate gifts and abilities that are intimately bound up with his/her consciousness.

Thus each single human being is unique – not only organically unique but also spiritually, for Transcendence Itself is embodied in him or her. His/her organic uniqueness is the instrument through which his/her spiritual uniqueness can function. This spiritual uniqueness, being Infinite-Eternal, is immutable. Since I, the self-conscious person, am in charge of the psycho-physical organism, it is my responsibility and duty to realize this organic uniqueness and orient it rightly apropos the spiritual uniqueness. Thus is orchestrated the divine symphony: the particular 'music of the spheres' which I am appointed by Transcendence to play.

How is this organic uniqueness realized? Listen to the bird singing. It sings naturally. It does not fly to an avian conservatoire; it pays no fees to another bird – a prima donna among birds. It just sings; song happens out of it. It is like the newborn baby, who just lives. It is that mysterious wonder, life, which makes the newborn grow.

Grow, then, as the newborn grows, as the flower grows. And remember the Upanishadic teaching: the body is the temple, the dweller in the temple is Shiva. Our task is to keep the temple pure, clean, whole, for it is sacred. Let no disharmonious thought or feeling sully the psyche, no improper act bruise the body.

Think too of musicians like Bach, Mozart, Beethoven, Chopin, Wagner, etc. Theirs was a musical consciousness. Their being and life, both outwardly and inwardly, cultivated and taught, intuited and inspired, transformed their consciousness – that is, their inner, invisible, non-descript 'knowingness' – into sublime music. This consciousness, which in itself is toneless, shapeless and formless, a 'knowing by being', *ex*-presses, that is, *puts out of itself* a structure in sound which we call music. So too, the expressions of the inner consciousness of those endowed with different gifts are called dance, poetry, painting, architecture, philosophy, etc. All these are cultural procreations. Procreation is true to type. Plants and animals reproduce themselves after their own kind – acorns do not produce apple trees, nor do sheep produce elephants. In the human sphere, the varied art forms – opera, symphony, lyric, sonnet, ode, drama, novel, painting, sculpture, etc., etc. – are each true to type.

Procreation belongs to the context of the finite and temporal, the mortal. Creation belongs to the context of the Infinite-Eternal, the immortal. Creation is absolutely transcendent – nothing like it elsewhere or before or after. And yet it is ceaseless action, constant newness, infinitely varied and wholly subsuming all procreation. Such is Transcendence.

•

Suppose an evangelist, a recruiting serjeant and a prosperous shopkeeper are travelling together on a bus. At the next stop ten youngsters are waiting. How will our three on board be conscious of them? Ten souls to be saved. Ten strapping recruits for our army. Ten willing pairs of hands behind the counter. Here are three different responses by three different consciousnesses.

Each person's inner consciousness determines his thoughts and feelings, speech and action. And thinking-feeling-speaking-doing influences his consciousness, which evolves according to the quality of his daily psycho-physical life. Its evolution is mainly in terms of intensity, inclusiveness, profundity, enlightenment and freedom. Each of these is interdependent and interactive with the others. Intensity is sensitivity and responsivity. If these grow there is inevitably greater inclusiveness and profundity, which spell greater enlightenment and freedom. The ordinary context of the functioning of subhuman consciousness is finitude and temporality. When this limited consciousness has evolved to the highest point possible for any human being, that consciousness can function in the context of infinity and eternity *in addition to* the usual subhuman context of finitude and temporality.

Such is holistic consciousness. It fully subsumes ordinary isolative and separative consciousness. If it did not it would not be possible to live safely and sensibly in a world replete with subhuman activity and the movement of machines. Even the perfected person has to be fully conscious separatively that he or she must not try to cross the road whilst a line of heavy vehicles is thundering past. If he or she were to try then they would have to forfeit any claim to good sense let alone to higher wisdom.

Holistic consciousness, the transmuted subhuman consciousness, marks the evolutionary fruition and perfection of *homo sapiens*. This sapience cannot be measured by the standards and values of the subhuman state. It is the wisdom, the omniscience, ascribed to God by the theist. Such an ascription would not be an instance of hubris. All descriptions of God are projections out of man's brain in superlative terms of what man himself has realized in holistic consciousness or aspired to realize as Transcendence's own fulfilment through him.

Man's statements about God's godliness are therefore ephemeral shadows of the Divine Reality. They change through the ages; but this changing panorama conveys the story of the evolution of man's consciousness from its primitive beginnings to its transcendent culmination. What is now transcendent for humans will be ordinary for the members of that more highly evolved race that some day will emerge out of the Infinite-Eternal into the temporal finitude.

The extremely few and rare ones who are fully-fledged *humans* are those in whom holistic consciousness can function freely as and when required.

•

The One Alone big-banged at the first dawn of the cosmos and so the Universe came into being. Before the last ray of sunset has faded, the Totality will return to the Origin, the One Alone.

One fertilized human cell becomes a hundred trillion living cells forming a marvellous co-operative system: a man, who is one alone. I am, just as you are, the One Alone. After fruition, emergence culminates in immergence back into the Origin. Emergence out of and immergence back into the One Alone belong to the context of infinity and eternity. Between emergence and immergence, evolution takes place, of which you, I and all individual one-alones are ordinarily conscious in the context of space-time. Spatio-temporal life, the shadow-play of eternal life, is the link between emergence and immergence. After the decoration of the deeps with matter and of the galaxies with light, evolution might have stopped had life not stepped onto the stage of existence. For life, the mysterious force uniting organism and consciousness (mind), ensures sensitivity, procreativity, and the continuity of the unavoidable struggle between the self-oriented separateness born of sense functioning and the urge for unification with all that seems other than self.

The resolution of that discord is through the realisation

of true individuality, which is also the discovery of one's own uniqueness. You, the one alone, and I, the one alone, are complementarily and not antagonistically different from each other. We are only different versions of each other and of the cosmos. Individual man, the microcosm, is as it were a unique holographic representation of the macrocosm: the Universe which is the body of Transcendence.

As in the macrocosm, dualism plays a powerful role in the life of the microcosm. Each and every person, male or female, is composed of both masculine and feminine elements. A man, though usually possessing predominantly masculine characteristics, also has feminine qualities; a woman, though predominantly feminine, has masculine traits. In every one there is the persona, the conscious aspect shown to and accepted by society; and also the shadow, the unconscious and repressed tendencies. The conscious and unconscious complement each other. In Jungian terms, the unconscious of a man has a complementary female element, his anima; that of a woman, a male element, her animus.

The story of man's organic descent is written in the structure of the brain. Like all his organs, the brain has evolved over millions of years, increasing in complexity and information content. Deep inside is the oldest part, the brainstem, which conducts the basic biological functions, including the rhythms of life: heartbeat and respiration. Capping the brainstem is the R-complex, the seat of aggression, ritual, territoriality and social hierarchy, which evolved over hundreds of millions of years in our reptilian ancestors; so, deep inside the skull of every human being is something rather like a crocodile's brain. Surrounding the R-complex is the limbic system or mammalian brain, which evolved tens of millions of years ago in mammals not yet arrived at the primate stage. Unlike the egg-laying reptiles, mammals gave birth to live young. The mammalian brain is a major source of moods and emotions and especially of loving care and concern for the young. Finally, on the outside, existing in uneasy truce with the more primitive brains beneath, is the cerebral cortex, which evolved millions of years ago in man's primate ancestors. The cortex is the instrument of intuition, critical analysis, ideas, inspirations, reading, writing, music, mathematics and man's whole cultural life. It is distinctive of the human species: the seat of humanity and the maker of civilization. Ever active, even in sleep, it pulses with the business of everyday life.

Science can investigate the processes taking place in the brain. Physics and chemistry can explain the mechanisms in the brains associated with sense functioning. But science does not discern any motive behind creation, any mind or guiding hand behind the evolutionary process. Mind can certainly intensify the knowledge of Nature, but science cannot show that mind has directed the operations of Nature.

The mechanism of the eye and the associated electrical activity in the brain are truly marvellous functions of energy. But what is the mental act which makes us say, 'I see a sunset'? How does the brain behind the eye 'see'? Physics and chemistry do not answer. The wonderful electrical activity in the brain can be examined, but no connection has been found between mind and energy. Yet brain and mind meet in the cortex.

Brain and mind are therefore different. Mind is immaterial; brain is material. Logic and reasoning belong to brain; revelation and unerring insight belong to mind. The forms of energy accessible to science *up to date*, may not be the sole forms of energy actually operating in the Universe. If there are subtler or transcendent forms of energy awaiting discovery, we may postulate Mind as that archetypal mode of functioning of the Primordial Creative Energy which is all-knowingness or pure consciousness. Primordial Creative Energy as Mind, stirred by the desire to manifest and know itself, sets going the involutionary concretizing process and the material Universe comes into being. Thereafter, the evolutionary process produces sensitivity, responsivity, life, memory, self awareness and analytic, discriminative consciousness, all of which characterize the material human body. Brain is the suzerain of the living organism. The living organism together with its brain is the apparatus or medium through which Mind may function. Mind, functioning freely through the organism, signifies that the imperfect subhuman has flowered as the fully-fledged human: as God. He is then true Incarnation.

'For man is truly God and God is truly Man,' said

Meister Eckhart (c.1260–1327/8), the Dominican theologian and greatest of German mystics, in his Ascension Day sermon entitled 'Hindrances'. Eckhart proposed this with special reference to Jesus Christ. Since there have been perfected holy ones throughout the centuries, it may be unequivocally said that Eckhart's words hold good potentially for every person. The Upanishadic sages affirmed 'Aham brahma'smi': 'I am Brahman'. Shri Krishna reveals to Arjuna: 'I am the Father of this Universe and even the Source of the Father. I am the Mother of this Universe, and the Creator of all' (B.G.9.17).

Brain functions and knows only in terms of duality: an observing subject and an observed object. Mind knows unitarily: by being what it knows. Thought is born of brain activity: a dualistic activity using speech as its medium of communication. Mind, pure consciousness, *is* the Reality, without needing concrete existentiality. Pure consciousness, revelation, subsumes brain and its reasoning without undergoing limitation of any sort.

As long as we are restricted to the subhuman state, our ordinary 'normal' state as we call it, we constantly experience the conflict between subhuman reasoning and truly human revelation, hence all theological and philosophical disputations, confusions and contradictions leading to wars, inquisitions, autodafés and all such bestial idiocies, instead of true clear-seeing of the fact as fact.

But how did the conflict between reason and revelation arise?

Reason versus Revelation

WE WILL CONFINE our consideration of the development of the conflict between reason and revelation to India and Europe, tracing the process from early days to the end of the 19th century.

Multitudes of devotees fervently believe that the Word of God as set out in their own scripture is the supreme and final revelation. Christians have the Bible, Muslims the Quran, Zarathushtrians the Gathas, Hindus the Vedas and the *Bhagavad Gita*. The Hindus, however, make a clear distinction between revelation, sruti, and authoritative tradition, smriti. Revelation comes from the founders of religions and those like them. They are the rishis, the singers of the songs of eternal life; the munis, the silent ones; the avataras, the incarnations of God (Sri Krishna was one): the great yogis and teachers of the Upanishads, like Yajñavalkya, Sanatkumara, Shakayanya, Pippalada and others. The Hindus freely concede that the founders of the world religions, like Zarathushtra, Gautama the Buddha and Jesus Christ, are manifestations of God. Frequently, these great teachers are themselves worshipped as God by multitudes, and this is regarded as quite natural and proper.

What was taught by the teachers is regarded as Truth, but we must understand the sense in which the word is used here. Not one of the great teachers formulated a theology or propounded a systematic philosophy. Each and every one of them spoke with authority from the Supreme by virtue of his own personal realization. They all declared that the Transcendent *Is*. They affirmed immortality. Each one of them taught a way of life by observing which a person could attain the bliss of the ineffable experience which we call the experience of God or the religious experience. The language in which each teacher couched his teaching was as perfect and beautiful an expression as was possible in the time and under the circumstances in which he lived. This teaching and that which was realized by living it is called the Truth by the followers of the teacher.

The religious life of the human race displays all grades from revelation's transcendental peaks to the low defiles of the crudest superstition. Religion in some form or other is part of the life of every human being, for essentially man is a religious being and only very secondarily a social, political and economic animal. Thus all the grades of religious activity are simultaneously operative in any society and are expressed in the forms acceptable to that society.

When in the long life of an ancient culture like that of India the religious life stagnates into mere observance of the forms of an ossified tradition, the spiritual tension so created evokes a new act of revelation. Therefore, as the inner reality of the Vedic revelation became gradually submerged under the rising tide of Brahmanic ritualism, the *Bhagavad Gita* emerged and the monotheistic forms of Hinduism: Vaishnavism and Shaivism. Buddhism came like a cold Himalayan wind, emphasizing reason. Shamkara and Ramanuja and the great systems of Indian philosophy made their contribution prior to and during the Christian era. After the incursions of Islam we see the rise of Sikhism.

Revelation is essentially and primarily an individual realisation. Love compels the Truth-finder, the God-realizer, to show others the way to the beatific fulfilment. A disseminative activity of communication arises between the Truth-finder and his personal followers. The master's own words are codified, a formal system is built up, and exposition after exposition of the teaching appears during the succeeding centuries.

The most intimate communication takes place when the rapport between master and pupil is perfect. How wonderful must have been those rare moments when a bhikkhu's mind was enlightened by the Buddha's wisdom! Or when a disciple of Jesus was enveloped by Christ's love! How transformed all the world must have seemed then!

But how grey must the same world have seemed when that radiance was dimmed by the pupil's inability to enlighten his neighbour or love his detractor. How unnerving to meet the shock of non-communication. How distressing to see that his exposition led farther and farther away from the heart of Truth. And if such things could happen with one who was in close proximity to the embodied revelation, how much more easily and surely would they happen to those even further removed from it.

Indians have been very individualistic where religion and philosophy are concerned. The Indian mind doubts, challenges and questions everything. In the *Rigveda,* the first great compilation of the spiritual texts of the Indo-Aryan peoples, the poet-seer asks in the last two verses of the famous Creation Hymn (10. 129. 6, 7):

> Who verily knows and who can here declare it,
> whence it was born and whence comes this creation?
> The gods are later than this world's production.
> Who knows then whence it first came into being?
>
> He, the first origin of this creation, whether he
> formed it all or did not form it,
> Whose eye controls this world in highest heaven,
> he verily knows it, or perhaps he knows not.

Or perhaps he does not know!

'God forgive this blasphemous doubter!' cries the devout unquestioning man of faith.

But it is precisely doubt – the right kind of doubt – which moves man to search for truth, whether it be in the sphere of Transcendence or of science.

Ancient Indian society was not composed solely of simple villagers. A vigorous, active, creative life surged through the Indian peoples from at least the days of the Indus Valley Civilization, which flourished long before the arrival of the Indo-Aryans sometime during the second millennium B.C. Matriarchies, republics, chieftaincies, monarchies and great empires have marked the vivid panorama of a subcontinent's history for thousands of years. Artists, intellectuals, philosophers, saints and mystics moved the currents of life through no unfruitful soil. Intellectual curiosity, religious awe, native wonder, inflexible devotion and a divine discontent all expended themselves in the creation of an aesthetic and spiritual culture whose full richness is at last beginning to be fully appreciated in our own day.

The spirit of agnosticism, an almost fierce scepticism, was certainly present in the Vedic hymns of the Indo-Aryans. The very existence as separate beings of the high gods – Agni, Varuna, Soma, Indra – was challenged. Thus, two great streams of divergent thought eventually emerged: (1) the Vedanta philosophy, which propounded the sole reality of Brahman, the non-duality of Atman and Brahman, and the illusory character of all manifestation; and (2) the Samkhya philosophy, which propounded universal evolution out of primordial nature or root matter, and postulated an infinite number of purushas (immortal human souls).

The sage Kapila, the reputed founder of the Samkhya philosophy in about the 7th or 8th century B.C., propounded an atomic theory as part of his philosophical speculations on universal evolution. He postulated Prakriti (the Unborn, Uncaused, Undying Energy) as the source of all manifestation. The fulfilment of the ends of Purusha is the cause of the three specialized states of matter (prakriti). In the evolutionary process there arise five subtle essences via intellect (buddhi) and self-sense (ahamkara), from which arise by preponderance of inertia the five gross elements, earth, water, fire (or light), air and ether, which are related to the five senses. A very interesting distinction is postulated between non-atomic all-pervasive ether and atomic ether.

Compare this with the ideas of the Greek philosopher Empedocles, who lived in the 5th century B.C.. His precursors Thales of Miletus, Anaximenes and Heraclitus had previously postulated water or the principle of moisture, air and fire as the origin of all things. Anaxagoras had meanwhile defiantly rejected all differences between the primary elements and the substances derived from them. Empedocles by contrast avoided a rigid 'this or that' view and comprehensively presented earth, water, fire and air as the four primary elements from which all substances are derived. Because Aristotle embodied these elements in his theory of Nature, the stamp of unimpeachability was placed on this doctrine for centuries. Again, Empedocles of Acragas, without using the methods of experimental chemistry, presented three fundamental conceptions: (1) the assumption of a limited plurality of primary elements, (2) the premise of combination in which such elements enter, and (3) the recognition of numerous quantitative differences or proportional variations of the said combinations.

Anaximander of Miletus postulated a single primal substance neutrally called Apeiron as the eternal, infinite, indefinite ground from which, in order of time, all arises and into which all returns. This bears some resemblance to the Prakriti of Samkhya philosophy. Similarly Plato says in his *Timaeus* (24): 'As to this mother and receptacle of things created. . . .we should not be at all wrong in calling it a certain invisible and shapeless essence, which receives all things and has a certain share of intelligence, though how is a matter very obscure and difficult of apprehension.'

Now, whereas Anaximander's world arises through a progressive differentiation, the Samkhya philosophy specifies a causal development. Cause is defined as the entity in which the effect subsists in a latent form: e.g. butter is the effect subsisting in milk, which is the cause. Development is the coming to light of what is latent. Aristotle would call it the transition from potential being into actual being; and Hegel, the passage from the implicit to the explicit.

But the Samkhya philosophy undermines the foundations of supernatural religion by substituting evolution for creation. It denies on the one hand that the Vedas are eternal, and on the other that they have personal authorship. They are regarded as self-evidently valid. Aware that other systems profess to be revealed, the Samkhya maintains that reason must be used to discover which codes of revelation are true and which not true. Aniruddha (Vritti) says: 'Only sayings supported by reason should be accepted'.

So the Samkhya philosophy, though it accepts the Vedas as canons of knowledge, discards many old dogmas and silently ignores others. Indeed, the second sutra of the *Samkhya Karika* of Ishvarakhrishna (3rd century A.D.)

states that knowledge derived from the revelation contained in the Vedas is ineffectual for deliverance from the bondage of existence. Here we see manifest the conflict between revelation and reason. And when in answer to Buddhism's challenge to realism the Samkhya developed on purely rationalistic soil and argued on strictly rational grounds, it was obliged to concede that there was no proof for the existence of God.

The Nyaya and Vaisheshika philosophies furthered the conflict by the use of this selfsame faculty of reason. The Nyaya offered conclusive proof for the existence of God; and both it and the Vaisheshika, in contrast to other speculative Indian philosophies which deal with the Universe as a whole, represent the analytic type of philosophy, upholding commonsense and science, and are distinguished by their critical treatment of metaphysical problems. Using the methods of logical enquiry and criticism, the followers of the Nyaya were willing to admit as true whatever can be established by reason. They dealt with the stock notions of philosophy – space, time, matter, causation, mind, soul and knowledge – explored their significance for experience and presented the results as a theory of the Universe. They attached great importance to free discussion, which is the life-breath of intellectual life. We are reminded here of Socrates and Plato, of Aristotle's 'Some see one side of a matter and others another, but all together can see all sides' (*Politics*), and of the praise of the method of free discussion in Milton's *Areopagitica* and in Mill's *Essay on Liberty*. Gautama (not the Buddha) like Aristotle systematised the principles of reasoning; his *Nyaya Sutra* tries to combine the results of the thought of the Brahmanas in the department of logic with their religious and philosophical dogmas, thus producing a logical defence of theistic realism.

The Vaisheshika philosophers propounded the view that the primary requirement of a sound philosophy is an analytic survey of objects which can be thought and named. The Vaisheshika categories – substance, quality, activity, generality, particularity, co-inherence and non-existence – seem to have been more strictly formulated than Aristotle's ten categories, for the Aristotelian analysis has been criticised by the Stoics and Neo-Platonists, by Kant and Hegel, as well as by Mill. The Nyaya theory of causation bears close resemblance to Aristotle's fourfold classification of causes: material, formal, efficient and final. The distinction between space and time is recognized in the Vaisheshika, and Shamkara Mishra (*Upaskara*, 2. 2. 10) holds that the relations of space are reversible whereas those of time are irreversible. We may compare this with Kant's Second and Third Analogies of Experience.

The Nyaya philosophers moreover hold mind to be a substance and atomic. Lucretius similarly propounded that the mind is composed of very subtle atoms; and John Locke postulated the soul to be a mental substance, a mental atom. The Nyaya view was that individual souls were eternal, manifold, perpetually separate from each other and distinct from mind and body, yet capable of apprehension, volition, desire, aversion, pleasure, pain, merit and demerit. Both the Samkhya and Nyaya philosophers postulated an infinite plurality of souls; but the Samkhya, unlike the Nyaya, regarded Purusha as attributeless. Whereas Kanada's *Vaisheshika* postulated atoms as different in kind, possessed of distinct individuality, primarily at rest and altogether different from souls, the Greek Atomists postulated atoms as having only quantitative and not qualitative differences (Democritus), as being in motion (Democritus and Epicurus), and as possibly constituting souls. Again, whilst the Greek Atomists developed a mechanical view of the Universe, the Vaisheshika view has a spiritual tendency, since the operation of moral law or dharma is central to the whole system.

The *Uttara Mimamsa* of Badarayana, better known as the *Vedanta Sutra*, sets out the philosophico–theological views of the Upanishads. It is not so much systematic philosophy as theological hermeneutic. The sutras, apparently unintelligible by themselves, leave everything to the interpreter. No less brilliant a constellation of thinkers than Shamkara, Bhaskara, Ramanuja, Baladeva, Vallabha, Vijñanabhikshu and others expounded this *Uttara Mimamsa*, each in his own way. Of these Ramanuja is the supreme champion of personal theism, Shamkara the unrivalled exponent of absolutism. Badarayana upheld a monistic view of the world, yet presented two views of Brahman: as personal lord and also as indeterminate intelligence. How can this be? Badarayana simply asserted it on the basis of revelation that Brahman develops Itself into the Universe but also remains transcendent. Similarly, in the *Bhagavad Gita*, we have Shri Krishna's affirmation: 'Having pervaded this whole Universe with one fragment of Myself, I remain' (10. 42).

The Buddhist religion, which arose out of the teachings of Siddhartha Gautama, known as the Buddha (c 566–486 B.C.), developed various branches within a thousand years of the Buddha's death. The Hinayana or Little Vehicle developed first, followed by the Mahayana or Great Vehicle, the Vajrayana or Adamantine Vehicle which enshrines the teachings of Buddhist Tantrism, and a few centuries later Zen evolved in China. In time philosophy and philosophies developed too, though the Buddha himself emphatically refused to talk about the ultimate foundation of things. His primary concern was with man's deliverance from suffering and he felt that philosophical speculation did not conduce to this deliverance, only the living of the holy life did. He therefore eschewed metaphysics. His followers were not so rigorous.

The Hinayana, one school of which, the Theravada, survives to the present, upholds the Arahant Ideal, an arahant being a practitioner who has trodden the Buddhist Way to its culmination in that ineffable state known as Nibbana or Nirvana, wherein all greed, hatred and delusion as well as the concomitant craving for existence as a separate self are utterly extinguished. The Mahayana, on the other hand, exalts the ideal of the bodhisattva: the altruistic practitioner who out of compassion postpones Nirvana so that he can return over and over again to the world to work for the alleviation of the suffering of others. Zen was a Mahayana refinement which sought to sweep away all the philosophical, legalistic and other accretions that had grown up around and obscured the simplicity of the Buddha's teaching over the centuries. Emphasising with characteristic directness the primacy of the Buddha's crucial enlightenment experience under the Bodhi Tree at Bodh Gaya, the Zen masters stressed the practice of intensive sitting meditation.

The Hinayana tradition is traditionally said to have spawned eighteen schools (in fact there were more) which produced their own Abhidharma (lit. 'Higher Dharma') or philosophical systematizations of the Buddha's teachings. For instance, the Sarvastivada or 'All-Things-Exist School', contrary to the Idealist thrust of many other schools, asserted a kind of naive realism, affirming that things can be said to exist in a real sense. It in turn spawned sub-schools, including the Sautrantika.

Within the Mahayana tradition, on the other hand, there emerged two very important schools of philosophy. Firstly, there was the Madhyamika or Central Way School founded by a South Indian philosophical genius named Nagarjuna (floruit c 150 A.D.). By the rigorous application of the dialectical method, all pairs of opposites are systematically negated and an elusive, inconceivable and ungraspable 'emptiness' or shunyata lying beyond them dynamically indicated. This school later spawned its own Prasangika (Dialectical) and Svatantrika (Dogmatistic) sub-schools. Secondly there was the Yogacara or Vijñanavada School, which emerged around the 4th century A.D.; Asanga and his brother Vasubandhu were its seminal masters. Central here was the doctrine of citta-matra or 'mind only': that all things are created by and from mind or consciousness. Further Mahayanist schools of philosophy developed in China, notably the Hua Yen (or Flower Adornment) and the T'ien-t'ai (or White Lotus) schools.

The realism of the Sarvastivada and its sub-schools has resonances in English Empiricism (John Locke *et al.*), Yogacara in Western Idealism (Bishop Berkeley *et al.*). The shunyata of the Madhyamika meanwhile reminds us of Hamilton's Unconditioned, Herbert Spencer's Inscrutable Power, the One of Plotinus, the Substance of Spinoza, the Neutrum of Schelling, and of the words of Duns Scotus, 'God is not improperly called No-Thing'. It has much in common with Shamkara's Nirguna (i.e. Attributeless) Brahman too – and yet, by a strange irony, the great exponents of Advaita Vedanta and Buddhist Madhyamika regarded themselves as supporting antagonistic doctrines!

•

In the attempt to explain the sensed world, atomic theories play a prominent part in the realistic approach. In such theories there is on the one hand the postulation of discrete entities called atoms, and on the other hand an all-pervasive, binding and unifying element or force called ether or akasha. Next, mind is given a higher value than matter. And in those philosophies which assert that Ultimate Reality is beyond mind and matter, self and not-self, this Ultimate is postulated in negative rather than positive terms.

We see that as the centuries pass reason plays an increasingly dominant role in all philosophical and scientific work. But the tendency has never been, except in a few cases such as the Carvaka and the Marxist philosophies, towards a totally materialist conclusion. Instead the urge has always been towards a transcendental reality: towards the ineffable culmination of a supreme religious experience. Reason and the logical processes of the discursive mind are therefore always subordinated to more profound modes of awareness of reality.

So one of the outstanding features of philosophy in India over the vast range of some 3,000 years has been an intimate relation with religion. Indeed, religion has both a more extensive and a more intensive meaning in India than perhaps anywhere else in the world. There philosophy and science have always been callow juniors to that venerable and all-benevolent parent, religion. Hence no revolt by reason against revelation brought about the break-up and downfall of the Indian House of Life and the creative spirit lived in India through many centuries. But for this very reason those special elements which are the very lustre of Western development, namely self-expressive individuality (not to be confused with rampant individualism) in the socio-political context and the development of the objective experimental method in the context of science, never developed in India as they did in the West.

In between the Western World and India stood Greece. Greece severed the ligatures of deep insight binding science and philosophy to religion. They survived to an extent in Western mysticism; also in those various cults which never achieved the healthy, finely charactered stature of true religion. Formal religion however degenerated into dogmatic theology and a rigid rule of moral living. Losing the clear awareness of its true nature, its purpose and its active place in life, it was increasingly marginalized while philosophy and science grew vigorously and, with characteristic adolescent unwisdom, romped the fields of life unguided by any wise parent.

It was necessary for this to happen. The faculty of reason had to develop to the limit of its potential and new means of approaching reality had to come to fruition. They have now done so. But in their growing up they have presented us with the modern world's conflict between reason, deemed to be the province of the scientist, and revelation, where the sage or seer is thought to hold sway.

What did Greece do?

Homer and Hesiod, coupled in Greek antiquity as the twin authors of Greek religion, stand in stark contrast. The personification of Nature supplied inexhaustible material for the play, first of imagination, next of imagination heightened to art. But the multiplicity of deities and myths surrounding Homeric man proved wearisome to the orthodox Greek. Hesiod of Ascra, Romanish among Greeks, pruned the luxuriance of epic poetry, reviving the immemorial but dimly understood traditions existing among the lower orders of Greece without respect to their claims to beauty. The unchecked imagination of Ionian poets, meanwhile, making light of the diversities and contradictions of legend, wandered widely from the methodical wisdom of the Boeotian peasant. The brilliant insouciance of their noble audience likewise diverged from the gloomy spirit of the countryfolk for whom Hesiod's poems were composed.

Hesiod's theogony is also a cosmology, for the origin of the gods included the origin of the world. Homer's Earth as the wife of starry Heaven, and Hesiod's Chaos, Gaia, Ouranos, Pontus, Titans and all the rest of the celestial and infernal host, bear resemblance to the pantheon of the *Rigveda,* though it must be remembered that the *Rigveda* antedates Homer and Hesiod by several centuries. As regards the origin of the world, Gaia and Eros appear at the beginning of the drama; the origin of Earth is then linked up with the origin of Chaos. Not a word of explanation regarding the when or the how of the process. It is very similar to the Austerity (or Fervour), Darkness and Love of the Creation Hymn, of the *Rigveda* (10. 129). But this is only natural, for myth and poetry invariably precede philosophy and science.

Now the Greeks were specially fortunate in their cultural heritage, for Chaldea and Egypt bequeathed them substantial scientific knowledge in the realms of geometry and astronomy. But the progress of science in Chaldea and Egypt was frustrated by the lifeless tenets of dogmatic religion. The Greeks, on the other hand, were again fortunate in lacking an organised priesthood. Thus with them begins the growth of science as observation of natural phenomena and as speculation about the origins and nature of the sense-perceived world. Having collected factual information, they theorized speculatively on the principles underlying phenomena. Two thousand years later, experimental science arose and developed in Western Europe.

The extension of natural science and of human dominion over Nature in ancient Greece produced two very important effects. First, in the religious sphere, the belief in the Universe as the playground of capricious, conflicting gods and godlings was undermined. Homeric polytheism slowly yielded the day to an ever-strengthening monotheistic feeling. And secondly, cosmogony began to free itself from theogony where the natural world was concerned, and matter became matter in its own right. Soon the Greeks were speculating whether Nature's multitudinous progeny issued from a prime matter rather than from Chaos – and once they set out on that track, they pressed home their pursuit. Like their Indian contemporaries, they conceived of the existence of elements and of the indestructibility of ultimate matter. But unlike their Indian counterparts, they did not sacrifice matter on the altar of spirit; instead they impounded it in the service of philosophy. They also exalted reason and the rational principle above everything. The manner in which they used reason in relation to science on the one hand, and to philosophy on the other, had a profound influence upon the theological formulation of the Christian revelation.

The Incarnation in Jesus is the culminating point of a very venerable religious tradition that harks back to Adam and Eve, Enoch, Methuselah and Noah. These figures stand like silent brooding peaks, reflecting the glow of an ancient spiritual light. Noah rides the Flood

– a flood of overwhelming inspiration which covers all the earth and makes indistinguishable all that had till then been known as separate, clearly-defined entity. The flood subsides and the generations of Noah and his sons, the families and nations, are divided across the Earth. But the whole Earth still has one language: the great sons of God, who, like Noah and others before him, still walk with God, still know the secret inner meaning of revelation. And then the Tower of Babel is made: the not-so-wise ones try to embody revelation in definite theological systems. Revelation can never be systematised; it can only be communicated in a flash by a look or a gesture, as when the Buddha held up a flower, Mahakashyapa gave a smile of recognition and Zen was born.

The fiery light of revelation confounded the speech of the builders of Babel so that they all fell into the sin of argument. So discord ever arises between revelation and subhuman reasoning.

More than 4,000 years ago Abram moved from Ur of the Chaldees to the Plain of Moreh and Egypt, and later came again to the land of Canaan and dwelt finally in the Plain of Mamre, which is in Hebron. This Abram, later called Abraham, the great Hebrew patriarch, was distinguished by an unsurpassable faith in one universal, invisible, omnipotent God, a unitary Being. This God is the foundation of the Jewish religion. The great figures of Moses amd Elijah, David, Solomon and the mighty prophets of Israel pass before our eyes till at last the gentle Galilean, that flaming sword of love, walks the earth. Jesus Christ is the embodied revelation of the Judaic Almighty God, the Word Made Flesh. And so was born the world of Christendom.

Jesus acknowledged that he was the Son of God; for that they crucified him. (We still do so by not living up to his teachings.) By his acknowledgement, the one God achieves full stature as the Loving Father. But he also becomes two: God the Father and God the Son. Moreover, the open tradition of the very patriarchal Hebrew people upheld a male God, with male archangels around him; and the canonical Gospels present a Jesus who speaks of and worships only a Father-God. This elevation of the male principle raised arguments among the children of men; again revelation was at war with reason. Saul of

Tarsus, a brilliant scholar who after his vision became Paul the profound mystic, took the process further. Paul was the first Christian theologian; his formulation is largely Platonic.

Plato, saddened and disgusted by the murder of Socrates by his Athenian judges, left Athens and travelled far and wide. Eygptian teachings and those of the Pythagoreans influenced him profoundly. Pythagoras had visited the Orient (some say even India), and celibacy and purity played no small part in his code. (The true significance of celibacy has not been understood in the development of the spiritual life. It is associated with the idea that woman, the seducer, is the obstruction to spiritual fulfilment.) Plato presented two 'ground principles'. One, the rational, formal principle; the other, the immediately apprehended, intuitive, emotional principle. The *Republic* investigates the rational principle; the *Symposium* and *Phaedrus* investigate the emotional aesthetic principle, eros, translated by Benjamin Jowett as 'frenzy', 'love', or 'passion'.

Plato brings these two principles together in the *Timaeus,* designating eros as the female or negative principle and the formal, mathematical, rational principle as the male principle. Quite arbitrarily this great philosopher stigmatized the female or negative principle, associated with materiality, the seen and known world, as evil. Conversely, the rational male principle, associated with the unseen, unknown God the Father, was the good.

Thus the ancients of East and West alike, failed to see that good and evil, male and female, seen and unseen, spirit and matter, are actually *complementary poles of one, unitary Whole*. Matter is the concretest manifestation of the Primordial Creative Energy, and spirit is the most subtle.

With Plato, philosophy – that is, general discussion between thinkers – ceased to be popular and became systematic. Since the coherence and strength of systematised philosophy are wholly dependent upon logical reasoning, the ratiocinative activity of the discursive mind accordingly assumed primacy. Here we see one powerful influence determining the theology of St. Paul. Another great influence was the Egyptian trinity of Serapis-Isis-Horus, which includes the female element, as does the analogous trinity of God-the Virgin Mary-Christ.

Another great influence was the Rabbinical, for Saul went to Jerusalem to study under the great Gamaliel, the grandson of that distinguished Jewish liberal, Hillel. The patriarchal influence of the whole Judaic tradition is seen in that other Christian trinity of God as Father-Son-Holy Ghost, despite the fact that, according to the Gospel of the Hebrews (which is really no less orthodox than the Four Gospels of the New Testament) Jesus says immediately after the Baptism, 'My mother, the Holy Ghost'.

The greatest influence on Paul was that of Jesus himself through his contact with Peter. Paul introduced the idea of a sacrificial person offered up to God as an atonement for man's sin. The man Jesus replaced the bull of Mithras. The Pauline system thus contains within itself the seeds of conflict.

In the 3rd century there flourished a definite school of Christian Platonism under Clement of Alexandria and Origen. In the 4th and 5th centuries the Church adopted Augustinian Platonism as Catholic orthodoxy. Finally, in the 13th century the Church also accepted Thomistic Aristoteleanism, more or less setting aside Augustine's work. The main influence for turning to an Aristotelean basis was Greek science. Aristotle rejected the Democritean–Platonic atomic theory and with it some of Plato's philosophical ideas regarding the unreality of the sensed world and the reality of the unseen. Aristotle identified the sensed world with the real world – therefore all ideas in the intellect are first given through the senses.

Aristotle profoundly influenced the intellectual development of the Western World and ineluctably that world came under the dominion of sense observation and discursive thinking; also of materialism, which arises when philosophy and science are cut adrift from mysticism. So Aristotelean science proved more acceptable than its Platonic antecedent and St. Thomas Aquinas reared the new theological structure of Catholic orthodoxy on the Aristotelean basis.

In the Aristotelean–Thomistic scheme, the soul of man is identified with the rational form of the living body and God with the rational form of the Universe, the word 'form' being conceived as a causal principle determining the growth and characteristics of the material body. St. Thomas and his followers were able to express the distinction between revelation and reason in completely Aristotelean scientific terms. Thus it is asserted that it is the function of revelation to make us constantly – that is, continuously – aware of the existence in perfection of the whole rational system or final cause of Nature, which human beings know only in part through rational science.

We can now appreciate how the rational principle rose to dominance in such a manner and to such an extent that theology, philosophy, science and the ordering of man's everyday life have all now come under its sway. To depart from the rule of reason would be tantamount to treason against God! And yet, for the unquestioning masses in Christendom, faith in the Word of God remains a naive faith in the literal word of the Bible, however much it is contradicted by scientific evidence or philosophical reasoning. For those who questioned deeply, however, revelation and reason, faith and fact, moved further and further apart – and the responsibility for this must undoubtedly rest with modern experiment science.

•

Greek science was, as we have seen, mainly observation of natural phenomena followed by speculation. But the rationale of modern experimental science is different. Firstly we have as complete and detailed an observation as possible of natural phenomena. Next we frame a hypothesis to explain these observations. (So far we are like the Greeks; but now we go further.) Assuming our hypothesis to be correct, we rationally deduce a,b,c,d, etc., and make certain predictions. Our next step is to devise laboratory experiments to test these. If the observed results tally, within acceptable limits of experimental error, with our deductions and predictions, we say that our hypothesis holds good so far. Thus we build up the edifice of our scientific theory. But if the results of our experiments contradict our predictions, we must revise or discard our initial hypothesis. Imagination or intuition is at play in obtaining the original idea, but it is formulated as a hypothesis only through the medium of reason and all subsequent evidence, whether positive or negative, is wholly subject to the authority of the rational principle.

The modern scientific method has transformed the world of philosophy, given birth to new cosmologies, shattered the old world of theology, brought discursive reason to the very frontiers of its domain, raised up rival authorities and flung a challenge to man to which the God-realizer himself must answer.

From Descartes onwards science obtained a stronger and stronger hold upon philosophy, slowly ousting the traditional influence of faith. Copernicus, Galileo, Bacon, Descartes and above all Newton founded the new science. Atomic theory was once again propounded and Aristotle repudiated. According to the new science, sensed qualities like heat, colour and sound were interpretations by the observer of different rates of vibration and did not reside in the external object. John Locke, philosophizing on this, presented man's body as composed of material atoms; his mind was a mental atom. He asserted that the only ideas a man can have are the simple ideas of sense data and the complex ideas which are associations of sense data. He did not however see that this made his doctrine of material and mental substances meaningless.

Bishop Berkeley demolished material substances. Hume exorcised the ghost of mental substances and the belief in the immortality of the soul. Leibniz and Kant showed that neither Locke nor Hume could account for mathematics and mathematical physics. Scientists trained in mathematics and especially the men who created the mathematics used in modern physics immediately saw the limitations of Locke's theory of ideas and the inadequacy of British Empiricism from Bacon and Locke through Hume and Bentham to Mill and Jevons. Moreover Newton had specifically distinguished the real mathematical space and time of physical science from that derived by sense awareness, to which Locke and Hume restricted knowledge. So a movement parallel to the philosophy of the Empiricists arose on the continent of Europe known as Continental Rationalism, its leaders being Descartes, Spinoza and Leibniz, all of whom knew more about physics and mathematics than Locke, Berkeley or Hume.

The evidence from three fields – mathematical physics, the moral life, and the development of historical institutions – shows that the Lockean and Humean scientific and philosophical conceptions of man and Nature are inadequate. Our knowledge, in terms of both commonsense and science, is composed of two parts: (1) that which is empirically observed by the senses, and (2) that which is theoretically postulated by reason. Immanuel Kant's great insight was just this: that not only our knowledge of mathematical physics but also our knowledge of commonsense objects involve a combination of sense data given purely inductively with an unsensed, rationally deduced and theoretically designated element. The world of things and persons is a synthesis of data received through the senses, which are contingent and empirical, and ordering and regulating concepts brought to the data by the knower, which are, said Kant, systematic, formal, universal and necessary. These concepts constitute Kant's *a priori knowledge*, consisting of the forms of sensibility, namely space and time, and the categories of understanding, such as substance, relation, causality, etc. Kant maintained that a priori concepts are the same for everyone, and he called the knowing self which brings these concepts to bear upon sense data the *Transcendental Ego*, which is the same for all differing persons, who are empirical egos or selves. The knowledge of one person by another was possible only through the Transcendental Ego.

It is the merit of Kant's philosophy and its derivatives that they transform modern man's conception of himself from a merely passive into a systematically active and creative being. There are flaws too, however. The Transcendental Ego tends in Hegel's Absolute to swallow up the empirical ego, leaving little or no meaning for freedom and independence of the concrete personality. This difficulty appears in the development of Kantian philosophy by Bradley and Bosanquet in England. Again, Kant was mistaken in conceiving the theoretic, rationally postulated component in knowledge as being categorical and necessary rather than hypothetical and confirmed only indirectly through its deductive consequences, as Vaihinger and Dewey have shown.

Deriving from Kant, Fichte propounded his dialectic logic of thesis, antithesis and synthesis, and his idea of the primacy of culture over Nature. His philosophy emphasized the primacy of the will and he even deduced the a priori concepts of Kant's *Critique of Pure Reason* from the single, solitary demand of the unconditioned will. Paradoxically enough, this philosophy, which begins in freedom, ends in determinism with Hegel and Marx. Hegel regarded Nature and culture as the unrolling through history of the free consciousness of the Absolute on its progress to self-consciousness; and the 'idea' as not merely regulative of human knowledge but as constitutive of the nature of things. Thus he arrived at his famous dictum: The real is the rational and the rational is the real. In ethics and social theory, Hegel and the Marxists identified the *ought* with the *is*.

The mistake made by these thinkers is that the negation of a thesis produces only one antithesis and that having done so the historical process becomes a predictable, determinate affair. Modern science has shown however that the negation of a thesis allows of more than one antithesis and that there is an element of chance as to which antithesis will react with which thesis. In short, there is the element of unpredictability.

Also, in none of the theories of natural scientists – Newton, Maxwell, Einstein, Max Planck – is Nature portrayed as obeying Hegel's dialectic. Modern science itself moved on, especially in the 20th century, with Einstein, Max Planck, Heisenberg, Schroedinger, De Broglie, Jeans, Eddington and others to experimentally verified theories of Nature quite different from those of Galileo and Newton. These revolutionary developments have of course spawned parallel developments in philosophy, including the outstanding philosophy of language of Ludwig Wittgenstein, which probes the outer limits of meaningful philosophical discourse: 'What we can't speak about we must pass over in silence' (*Tractatus Logico–Philosophicus*, proposition 7).

So, with the advance of modern scientific knowledge, the old cosmologies of theologians and speculative thinkers are being discarded, and faith in the revealed word of God as presented by theologians has been shaken to its foundations. Modern psychology meanwhile compels us to revise all our old views about man's nature, and psychical research is investigating paranormal faculties of the mind not investigated hitherto. Most significantly science has demonstrated that all our investigations to date can only give us grounds for holding a hypothesis, not for absolute certainty; next, that what we call established facts are merely mental constructs; and lastly, that we are now beginning to step beyond the frontiers of discursive mind, within which alone what we have been accustomed to call logical reasoning has meaning.

In his great work, *Tractatus Logico–Philosophicus*, Wittgenstein adumbrates the powerful image of his own propositions collectively serving as a kind of ladder to take the reader up to a point where he must kick the ladder away and proceed beyond by some as yet unknown mode of inquiry (proposition 6.54). Here we have a philosopher propounding a philosophy that internally articulates the necessity of its own transcendence.

But as the old world crumbles, what undiscovered country lies ahead?

Holistic Consciousness and its Context

THE WHOLE STORY of the cultural development and history of mankind is the story of the animal species *homo sapiens*. Almost every past and present member of this species, with very rare exceptions, was and is isolatively and separatively self-conscious. He or she, the living organism, is the self; the rest of the Universe beyond the boundary limits of his or her skin is the not-self. Presumably the members of various other animal species are similarly conscious.

The relationship between self and not-self is not one of unity or harmonious order but of conflict and disorder. Some selves struggle hard and bend their efforts to produce harmony; but pure harmony emerges only out of effortless action. If the means do not embody harmony, the end will certainly not be harmonious because means invariably build themselves into ends. (The house built of faulty bricks must fall down sooner or later.) Only right means, not *any* means, justify good ends.

We, the innumerable multitude, are still sub-human; but we are growing, albeit very slowly, towards fully-fledged *human-ness*. Evolution has brought the human body to its present pitch. In about a score of years after birth, Nature completes her task of maturing the body. The maturing of the psyche, on the other hand, is each person's own responsibility, assisted during childhood and adolescence by parents and educators.

Parents and educators bear a colossal responsibility. If by and large man is still an unfinished animal, how many parents and teachers are fit for their vocation? This far more than poverty or disease is our most serious problem. Insecurity, illness, wars, evil-doing and the whole host of human problems and miseries are the consequences of man's ignorance of his own nature, of where he is going, of the purpose(s) of his existence and of how to fulfil them.

From birth onwards, every sensation determines the child's awareness of his environment. Ideally, let him be brought up in an atmosphere of love, with gentle care and amid peaceful surroundings. Thunderstorms are of course beyond the parents' control; so too the roaring of lions if you live in lion country. Freedom from fear is very important throughout all the years up to independent adulthood. Childhood is a period of special psychical sensitivity to the 'atmosphere' created in the home by the parents and other members of the family.

The nature of the child's consciousness of life and its ways finds expression in his behaviour. As the years pass, daily experience and accumulating knowledge gathered from outside himself and resulting from his own observation, experimentation and thinking produce changes in his consciousness of both his self and the not-self.

It is very important to feed his sense of wonder about everything, to encourage him to explore and find out things for himself, to doubt and not be gullible or reject things out of hand. He should be encouraged to consider carefully for himself and not be passively conditioned by authority, though of course he can't debate with the inexorable facts and realities of existence. Above all, encourage him to keep an open mind, always inquiring, always testing in order to find out the truth.

Perhaps the heaviest responsibility of parent and teacher is to help the child to understand true virtue and to live virtuously. The bribery of heavenly rewards and threats of hellish punishments and tortures are all stupid and useless in this connection. The carrot (of heaven) and the fire (of hell) have been tried for several thousand years and have proved an abject failure in making humanity virtuous, for the human race today is almost as dedicated to evil-doing and inhumanity as in its so-called savage and primitive beginnings. The human leopard does not seem to have changed more than a spot or two! And yet there has been change, for people are now much more conscious of evil and horror than in past ages.

What has been and will always be the great educative influence for virtuous living? It is the living example of virtue in parent, teacher and friend as well as in the great exemplars of both past and present. There is that in most human beings which instinctively thrills in favourable response to the nobility and beauty of virtuous living – which is the vital reality of religious and truly human living.

Living virtuously is the most powerful influence for transforming man's nature, for purifying his psyche of fundamental ills such as greed, hate, delusion, fear, suspicion and all associated stupidities.

Each man, by virtue of the fact that he is unique – there is no one else in the world quite like him – must carve out his own path and tread it like a true hero so that the fruitive culmination of his virtuous living is the transmutation of his usual separative and isolative consciousness into the beacon of holistic consciousness.

•

Two main drives characterize the organic world: self-preservation and the preservation of the species. It is difficult to decide whether these drives are motivations of consciousness or not. A new-born baby hardly knows that it exists. It cries. The mother puts it to her breast and there is a vigorous action for taking in the sustenance necessary for preserving life. So too with elimination. Pleasure is associated with both ingestion and excretion, which the infant announces with happy sounds. Conversely, should any difficulty or painful obstruction be experienced, the infant cries to express its discomfort and displeasure. After birth, sensory life gradually strengthens, as does conscious discrimination between pleasurable and unpleasant sensations: between what is acceptably 'good for me' and what is 'bad for me'.

Forms of sensory life also exist before birth. The moment of quickening, the incipient travel within the womb by the unborn, is a conscious delight to the mother, who clearly knows what it means. She has fulfilled her womanhood by promoting life and by furthering the species. The unborn one has also floated in a little ocean of life and heard the vital rhythms of the mother's heart-beat and the streaming of her blood. Touch and hearing, feeling and listening – what wonderful mysteries are experienced before we are born! And, after the massive struggle to emerge out of the old, enclosed, lightless world into the totally different new world, the baby utters his first cry, which is both a victorious vaunt of liberation and an expression of tremulous fear and defiance of the entirely strange new world of air and light into which he has been summarily precipitated. However, he has the consolation of the touch of mother's flesh and the sound of her loving voice: rich compensation indeed for the absence of the sound of her heart-beat and rushing blood.

The new-born baby is of course unconscious of the fact that he has achieved all this at the expense of shedding his mother's blood. Insofar as the mother represents the basic materia of all existence, this constitutes his first sin: his first violation of the unity of the Universe. This is *weltschmerz:* the suffering of the world. Has the sin to be expiated by the sacrifice of his own life? In its true sense, 'sacrifice' means 'making sacred', which means making holy, restoring wholeness. But how is this to be done? Only by giving oneself freely to Totality. It must, however, be a pure gift – pure both physically *and* psychologically: that is, pure in mind, pure in consciousness.

Purity of body is easily enough contrived: eat fresh, unadulterated food – grain, vegetables, fruit, nuts, herbs – and do not kill for food or cause any innocent animal, fish or bird to be killed,, for then you become an accessory after the fact. Do not say, 'You kill plants when you gather them for the pot.' When ripe, grain must be harvested and fruit picked or else it rots.

The Bible says:

> And God said, Behold, I have given you every herb-bearing seed, which is upon the face of all the earth, and every tree in which is the fruit of a tree yielding seed; to you it shall be for food. (Genesis, 1.29).

And the Hindu scriptures echo:

> The foods that augment vitality, energy, vigour, health, joy and cheerfulness, delicious, bland,

substantial and agreeable, are dear to the pure. (B.G. 17.8).

So too with drink: take infusions, the juice of ripe fruit and pure water (the 'unbrewed ale' on which Adam and Eve thrived so well). The sacred texts of many religions advise the avoidance of alcoholic drinks which befuddle the mind and make keen awareness impossible.

Give the body proper exercise. Walk, run, swim, dance, climb; play games and do what is necessary for your particular body to keep fit. Enjoy – but be moderate. It is sad to see the body being mercilessly driven beyond its normal endurance levels for the ego-serving vanity of breaking records or out of greed. Therefore, enjoy sport for its own sake; do not glory in competition. Victory is always extracted at the expense of another or others. To lose is always bitter, while to win inflates the ego and makes it hard and selfish.

Give the body due rest. Whenever possible, enjoy the beauty and healing peace of Nature, all your senses alert, either alone or in suitable company. Also keep the body scrupulously clean. Choose your companions very carefully as well: bad companions can lead to all kinds of complicated, sometimes even disastrous situations.

•

The living human body is not just matter in solid, liquid and gaseous forms. It is psycho-physical. The dead body is devoid of psyche, which is a sensitivity or form of 'energy' associated with the characteristic of livingness. The cells of the dead body have lost their usual powers – self-motivation, self-reproduction, self-healing.

What is psyche? It is not exclusively Mind, that archetypal mode of functioning of the Primordial Creative Energy which is all-knowingness or pure consciousness. Stated this way, we are postulating Mind, or Mind Power, as a transcendental energy not amenable to scientific investigation. This transcendental energy is non-descript, characterless in itself, universal. It does not light or heat anything, attract or repel, expand or contract anything. Nevertheless because of it there is law and order, growth (non-physical), development and fulfilment intellectually and spiritually for any particular being and for Total Reality. It is transcendental intelligence which guides all change and transformation by virtue of its actual being, its presence, not by premeditated planning, which is Mind's shadow in the human sphere. (God has no plan for the Universe; God is ceaseless creative action; and Mind is God's formative agent of universal process.)

Postulating mind in this way as a transcendental energy different from all energies known to science and not as yet open to scientific investigation would probably be unacceptable to the orthodox scientist. He would quite likely say – and quite justifiably – 'All this is dogmatic affirmation unsupported by solid evidence.' Quite so. But is it not in the very nature of ontological presentation to affirm axioms that appear self-evident to the person affirming them? Of course there is no 'proof' for such axioms. Man may some day experience their reality *if they are true*, but the writer has no option under existing circumstances than to state what comes to him, keeping an open mind and waiting patiently until proof or disproof is forthcoming.

I sit at my familiar desk, typing these words. My sensory experience convincingly 'proves' to me that my typewriter is made of solid matter. Twentieth century science equally undeniably assures me that 'matter' is actually a series of patterns out of focus. The search for the ultimate stuff of the Universe ends with the discovery that there isn't any! I like that and I accept both 'undeniables', for I maintain that it is a question of which mode of consciousness is functioning at the moment. Is it holistic consciousness? Or everyday consciousness limited by sense-brain functioning? So I stand equally by scientific assurances and by 'what comes to me' ontologically. Sunshine both ways!

Science has investigated the forms of energy we experience in our daily life: electrical, magnetic, photic (light), thermal, chemical, gravitational, mechanical, nuclear. Would a conscientious scientist be likely to declare: 'We have examined all the forms of energy there are and can therefore categorically assert that no other forms exist'? Surely not. There may well be subtle forms of energy awaiting discovery. Therefore, although science has not yet found any cross-connection between Mind and the energy concept, it may do so in the future. In any case, we know from our own life-experience that mind is a power, and a remarkable one at that, though in this context the word 'mind' should rightly be replaced by 'psyche'.

We have stated that Mind is universal. That which is universal, like space for instance, cannot be split up into chunks, one of which any of us might appropriate for himself. In the same way, I, the finite organism, cannot possess or contain Mind. Mind-energy, interacting with matter – in our case the living body – gives rise to psyche, which is rooted in the brain and nervous system and is powerfully influenced by the activity of the ductless glands, the condition of the blood and the general state of physical health. Psyche is partially physical, partially metaphysical: a child of Father Mind and Mother Matter. Psyche and body are in intimate communion in the living psycho-physical organism. Thought and feeling, intellect and emotion, are all psychical (not mental) expressions of the living individual. I cannot say I have a mind, but I can say I have my own psyche just as surely as I have my own heart, lungs, hand or foot. The psycho-physical organism is in fact a distinct and particular whole; so is every other such organism. Thus each and every person is unique. He or she is different from everyone else in character, separate from all else as a manifested object, but *not* unrelated to any and every other person or object in the Universe, for with any and every one of them he or she interacts, even if unknowingly, to the farthermost reaches of space and time.

Sadly, with very rare exceptions man is not conscious of his inextricable inter-relationship with Total Reality. This unconsciousness is the root of the abysmal ignorance from which he suffers: the fundamental avidya or 'not-seeing' which causes the tragic split between self and not-self.

As long as we are in good health, we are conscious of the body as a one-thing, a unitary whole. If anyone asks, 'How are you?', the answer is, 'I am fine.' This is holistic consciousness as far as the body is concerned. If some illness afflicts the body, that afflicted part causes a loss of consciousness of the unitary wholeness of the body. We become acutely conscious of the ailing part at the expense of the whole. When healed and restored to right relationship then once again 'I am fine'.

Many people can entertain the thought that the Universe is a unitary whole. But although they may cling tenaciously to the idea, they are not fully conscious of it. Holding a thought or belief or idea in the mind is different from being fully conscious. That of which you are truly conscious expresses itself naturally and spontaneously through all your thinking, feeling, speaking and action. How did you think and feel and speak and act when you were really in love – *really* in love, not merely infatuated or merely conditioned by popular conceptions of how love 'ought' to be expressed? Love transcends all fixations. Its expressions are invariably and inevitably perfectly beautiful and pure. The rose of genuine love is not spiked with the thorns of possessiveness, jealousy, exclusivesness or selfish demands. It grows on the delicate stem of harmlessness. Its open-hearted perfume transforms turbulent world-woe into tranquil happiness. It is the loveliest gift of holistic consciousness to all creation.

Holistic consciousness is not something which can be acquired or attained as a goal by an aspiring seeker. As explained earlier, only if we pay fine attention to our sense-impressions do we become conscious of that to which we pay attention. In our daily life we react to our sense-impressions in terms of like and dislike, acceptance or rejection, approval or disapproval etc., according to our psychological conditioning and/or the unavoidable conditioned responses of the body to danger. This last is essential for the well-being of the body. Careful observation of our reactions tells us what we are like.

If we look at our sense-impressions and at our thinking processes, at our beliefs, ideas, convictions, etc., with a pure looking *and nothing else* – an arduous task! – there comes the stage when such bare observation is entirely free of all conditioned reactions and then indeed we are conscious of the fact as the fact, pure and simple – that is, holistically.

Holistic consciousness is free – and this is the essential crucial point – of reaction for or against that of which we are conscious. Only then can we make a pure response in terms of right action, which is action entailing no ill consequence. Such bare observation in holistic consciousness is not indifference nor is it self-centred in any way. It is observation by the truly selfless man. It stirs one transcendentally – and then one's response will embody the great spiritual values: truth, love, wisdom, goodness, purity, beauty, all of which are healing powers. So in holistic consciousness we are in communion, in harmony with the Totality. Pure, bare observation in holistic consciousness is impartial with the impartiality which characterizes perfect justice.

Holistic consciousness rejects nothing whatsoever. It never refuses to attend to any event or impression that comes to it. Being free of personal conditioned reactivity, the holistically conscious person can understand everyone and everything, which means that he sees the truth of all experience and things. Whoever sees the truth is able to heal, make whole, restore to holiness. All the perfected holy ones who have graced and do grace our world have had healing powers, for holistic consciousness can utilize transcendent energies still unknown to all of us who are still subhuman.

Isolatively and separatively self-conscious man, that is the innumerable multitude, confined to the context of finitude and temporality, does not know the freedom of the fully-fledged, holistically conscious *hu-man*. The manifest Universe of space-time offers no obstruction to him. But his is not a freedom in the sense of doing what he likes, for it is only the isolative and separatively conscious 'I' that has preferences. This, the plague befouling immature man and his environment, is the very antithesis of that true freedom which begins with intelligent self-restraint having transcended all suppression. The fully-fledged human is devoid of all likes and dislikes and of the tyranny of all duality. He swims with the current of life as it flows towards fruition. Transcendence lays no yoke upon him for Transcendence has no need to compel or even to persuade. Patience is infinite in the transcendent context of the Infinite-Eternal. The Law (Rigvedic Rta, Avestan Asha, Buddhist and Hindu Dharma), the Divine Ordinance, happily guides and inspires the holistically conscious man to act and be in harmony with Transcendence, even as the ring dance of atoms displays the marvel and beauty of the cosmos.

Holistic consciousness is a cosmic consciousness.

Insofar as it rejects nothing but observes everything, it is God-consciousness. There is no cosmic dustbin waiting to be filled with the rejects of the cosmos. There can be no rejects in the Infinite-Eternal, for under the beneficent gaze of those sleepless immortal eyes everything is transformed into divine perfection. Transcendent love and wisdom transmute all ill into the altogether well.

All this is not far away. It is in the absolute *here-now* of the Infinite-Eternal. To us, the children of mortality, there is the invisibly minute and the unimaginably boundless, but to the son or daughter of immortality there is Totality in the twinkling of an eye. Eternity is not a 'for ever and ever': the terrible boredom of an endless temporality. All that we mortals mean by a dead past and a beckoning future is embodied in a never-born, never dying, ever present *now*: a secret stillness which is the ceaseless pulse of creation – life/new life, mysteriously not an other life but the One Eternal life. Eternity spells the instantaneous birth-death of time, which is the dance of life to our ordinary limited consciousness.

Holistic consciousness of the Infinite-Eternal negates all our interpretations of the meanings and significances of all that of which we are conscious in terms of the finitude and temporality without destroying the finite and temporal. If it did so there would be no bridge for us mortals to the sphere of the immortal. Such is the mercy of Transcendence: *the finite and temporal is completely subsumed in the Infinite-Eternal*. So marvellous is the love and wisdom of Transcendence that here and now in the mortal realm we can experience immortality. For where there is no separation or isolation of ordinary consciousness, we transcend time – and therefore sorrow, becoming, birth and death – and realize timelessness, which is a foreshadowing of eternity, though not identical with eternity.

The experience of timelessness begins at a moment in time and ends at another moment in time. Every experience, however transcendent, has to have a beginning and an ending, because the psycho-physical organism has to return to its ordinary bodily state to feed, rest, etc., or else it would die. Whilst we exist materially as a specific organism we have to submit to the laws of organic existence therefore.

However, even though temporally bounded, eternity's touch of grace is filled with ananda or indescribable bliss. This bliss is not ecstasy, however intense, or mere happiness; it is devoid of sensation. It is more an ineffable, still and silent peace beyond all human conceiving or understanding.

•

Since the person in holistic consciousness is at home in the context of infinity and eternity, he can act as a conduit for the healing or whole-making power of the Primordial Creative Energy. This gives us insight into the pheonomenon of so-called spiritual healing and the healing miracles performed by the perfected holy ones.

The psyche, brought into being by the interaction of Mind-energy with the material body, is responsible for giving rise to isolative self-consciousness: the 'I-am-I and not anyone or anything else' idea – an idea and mode of consciousness, which disappear completely on the disintegration of the organism at bodily death. In profound dreamless sleep also this isolative self-consciousness vanishes; but on waking, the separative 'I-am-I' idea reasserts itself with the resumption of the activity of the vigilance centre in the brain. The separative I-idea and all beliefs and thoughts derived from it – such as 'I, exclusively, am the doer or maker of this act or thought or object', etc. – are illusions.

This is where the popular conceptions of karma are inadequate and misleading. No one is *exclusively* responsible for his own and everyone's thinking-feeling-speaking-doing in the world. Since all the particulars composing the Universe are interactive and inter-related, each is responsible for all and all are responsible for each. Furthermore, ideas of any *separate permanent identifiable entity* preceding birth and surviving death are illusions. The One Primordial Creative Energy becomes the countless particular entities, all of which resolve into the Origin after having played their part in universal manifestation.

When the psyche is purified, emptied of all illusions, beliefs, prejudices, assumptions and preconceptions, then universal and transcendent Mind-Power functions freely through the psycho-physical organism, the person.

It is a creative power which can heal – make holy. If a 'sinner' (he with a sick psyche) genuinely repents – that is, turns away completely from his 'sin' in consciousness – his psyche is ready to be filled with the creative healing power of Mind. The perfected holy one or healer does not wish or think, 'May so-and-so be free of his stomach ulcer.' Entering into holistic consciousness, he concentrates his attention upon Truth, the holy state, which is transcendentally healthy, and thereby suffuses the 'sinner' with this consciousness. If true repentance by the 'sinner' has taken place, the transcendent healing energy of Mind will of itself effect the miracle.

Such healing has been called faith-healing. The healing miracles by Jesus are well-known. Not so widely known are examples of healing mentioned in different scriptures. To cite one example: in the *Sanyutta Nikaya* (The Collection of Kindred Sayings, 5.381 ff) of the Buddhists, it is told how the wealthy householder Anathapindika, a benefactor of orphans, loyal devotee of the Buddha and a generous supporter of the Sangha (the Order of Buddhist monks and nuns), fell seriously ill. He sent a messenger to Sariputta, one of the foremost disciples of the Buddha, to beg him in all compassion to come to his sick bed. Sariputta complied and came with Ananda, the Buddha's lifelong attendant.

Hearing that the sick man's pains were increasing, Sariputta enumerated Anathapindika's virtues and said to him, 'If you were to think of your unswerving loyalty to the Buddha, your pains would be allayed in a moment.' He repeated this twice more, substituting 'Dhamma' and 'Sangha' for the word 'Buddha', then added that, unlike the ignorant masses, Anathapindika had right knowledge and right release. On all these counts, Sariputta assured Anathapindika, his pains would be allayed in a moment.

'Thereupon,' says the text, 'in a moment the pains of the householder Anathapindika were allayed.'

Other statements in the Buddhist texts can be similarly understood. For instance, in one place the Buddha tells King Ajatasattu that one of the fruits of living the life of the holy recluse is that 'with the heart [the mind or psyche] made pure, serene, translucent, cultured, devoid of evil, supple, ready to act, firm and imperturbable, he applies and bends down his mind to the modes of the wondrous gift and enjoys it in various ways – being one, he becomes many, or being many he becomes one again; he becomes invisible or visible; he goes feeling no obstruction to the further side of a wall or rampart or hill, as if through air; he penetrates up and down through solid ground as if through water; he walks on water without breaking through as if on solid ground; he travels cross-legged in the sky like a bird on the wing,' etc.

'With his heart thus serene,' etc., the text goes on, 'he applies and bends down his mind to the heavenly ear [clairaudience]. With that clear heavenly ear, surpassing that of men, he hears sounds, human and celestial, whether far or near. Similarly, with respect to the heavenly eye [clairvoyance], surpassing that of men, he sees beings as they pass away from one form of existence and take shape in another. He recognizes the mean and the noble, the well-favoured and the ill-favoured, the happy and the wretched, passing away according to their deeds and reaping the consequent fruit [heaven or hell]. Furthermore, penetrating the hearts of others with his own heart [serene, pure, etc.] he discerns the passionate mind to be passionate, the calm mind to be calm, the angry. . . peaceful. . . dull. . . alert. . . attentive. . . wandering. . . broad. . . narrow. . . mean. . . lofty. . . free. . . and the enslaved mind to be enslaved.'

Similarly it is said in the Christian Gospels of Jesus that he knew what was in the mind of others. For instance, the Gospel of John (4.7–11) tells us that whilst Jesus was sitting near Jacob's Well by the Samaritan town of Sychar, a woman came up to draw water. Jesus said to her, 'Give me a drink'. She was surprised that a Jew should ask a drink from a Samaritan. After a little talk, Jesus said, 'Go home, call your husband and come back.' She answered, 'I have no husband'. 'You are right,' said Jesus, 'in saying that you have no husband, for, although you have had five husbands, the man with whom you are now living is not your husband; you told me the truth there.' She replied, 'Sir, I can see that you are a prophet. . . '[1]

Again, Jesus walked on the waters, commanded storms to subside, brought the dead back to life, gave eyesight to

[1]Other instances are to be found in Matt. 9.4; 12.15,25; 16.8; 26.10. Mark, 2.8; 8.17. Luke, 5.22; 6.8; 9.47; 11.17. John, 2.25; 6.64.

the blind, etc.; he could also make himself invisible (John, 8.59; 10.39). As such psychic powers were also possessed by the great Hindu rishis and yogis, one wonders whether Jesus ever went to India[1].

In one of the Rigvedic hymns to Soma, the god of inspiration, we have the following verse (8.68.2):

> All that is bare he covers over, all that is sick he medicines:
> the blind man sees, the cripple walks.

In our own day too there are records of actual physical healings, as at Lourdes; also by the great modern sage J. Krishnamurti[2].

The perfected holy ones, holistically conscious, affirmed their union with God or their realization of truth, in various ways:

> Pragatha: We have drunk Soma and become immortal; we have attained the light; the gods discovered.
>
> (RV.8.48.3)

> Zarathushtra: When I beheld Thee in my very eyes, then I realized Thee O Mazda, as the First and Last of all Eternity.
>
> (Ys.31.8)

> Jacob: I have seen God face to face and my life is preserved.
>
> (Gen.32.30)

> And Enoch walked with God: and he was not for God took him.
>
> (Gen.5.24)

> And Moses went up unto God, and the Lord called him out of the mountain.
>
> (Exod.19.3)

[1]See *Jesus died in Kashmir*, A. Faber-Kaiser, London, 1977, and *Jesus lived in India*, Holger Kersten, Shaftesbury, 1986.

[2]See *Krishnamurti, a Biography*, Pupul Jayakar, San Francisco, 1986, pp. 204–206.

> And the Lord spake unto Moses face to face, as a man speaketh unto his friend.
>
> (Exod.33.11)
>
> The Buddha: Monks, there is a not-born, a not-become, a not-made, a not-compounded. Monks, if that unborn, not-become, not-made, not-compounded were not, there would be no release from this here that is born, become, made, compounded.
>
> (Udana, 80)
>
> Jesus: I and my Father are one.
>
> (John, 10.30)
>
> Believe me I am in the Father and the Father in me.
>
> (John, 14.11)
>
> Shri Krishna: I am the abode of Brahman, the Immortal, the Inexhaustible, of eternal righteousness and unending bliss.
>
> (B.G. 14.27)

For a more detailed listing see *The Heart of Religion*, by P.D. Mehta, Shaftesbury: Element Books, 1978 (new edition 1987), pp. 15–21.

•

Ordinarily, when we talk of evolution we mean the process of formation and the development of any creature. It is a continuous genetic adaptation of organisms or species to the environment by the integrating agencies of selection, hybridization, inbreeding and mutation. Thus we talk of the *evolution* of man, or of a particular organ such as the brain, as we have done in earlier chapters. Each organ has some specific function.

To be conscious is to be inwardly awake to something. It always includes being awake to oneself as the experiencing and perceiving subject, and paying attention to some thing or event external to oneself, or which is internal, such as one's own sensations, cognition, emotions or thoughts.

'Conscious-ness' is a word signifying that wakeful,

knowing state of mind present when the whole complex of attention, object, event or action is taking place. Consciousness is a *state of knowing-ness*, not a material organ. Nevertheless it can change: 'expand' or 'grow' or undergo transformation or transmutation. It can reach a culminating point (as happened with the perfected ones) dependent upon the sensitivity of the organism and its environment. The organism is the indispensable apparatus through which the transmuted consciousness functions. It is therefore not strictly correct to speak of the evolution of consciousness, only of it changing in the direction of that fruitive culmination which we call holistic consciousness.

Holistic consciousness is not 'attained' or 'achieved' by a holy one. It supervenes when the organism, purified and well-prepared to sustain the action of transcendent energies, is in a properly receptive state; that is, when it offers the right conditions for ordinary everyday consciousness to change into holistic consciousness. A bud does not 'attain' or 'achieve' anything when it flowers. It undergoes a natural transformation out of the bud-state into the flower-state. So too holistic consciousness represents the full flowering of a human being. And just as the flowering of a bud *happens*, so too flowering of the person into fully-fledged human-ness *happens*. To strive to attain, to try to storm the ramparts of heaven, would be quixotic. Simply be good, naturally and happily, and the *best* will make you its place of rest (Sabbath). In holistic consciousness you are *at-oned* within Transcendence. And since Transcendence is always blissfully creative – not merely pro-creative – you the fully-fledged human are a blissful creator.

When Christ went into the Mount to pray, when the great mystics entered the contemplative state, when the Buddha or any perfected holy one entered meditation, the man Jesus, the man Gautama or whoever he was *underwent refreshment*. He was bathed in the water of the spirit; he was burnt in the fire of creation; he was inspired by the light of divine wisdom. And then he went out amongst his fellow men and women as the emissary of the Most High.

> Know ye not that ye are the temple of God, and that the Spirit of God dwelleth in you?
>
> (1 Cor. 3.16)

> What? know ye not that your body is the temple of the Holy Ghost which is in you, which ye have of God, and ye are not your own?
>
> (1 Cor. 6.19)

In the *Maitreya Upanishad* and *Skanda Upanishad,* the teacher declares:

> The Body is the temple. The dweller in the temple is Shiva.

All this is realized – *realized,* not merely *thought of* or *believed* or *hoped for* – in holistic consciousness in the context of infinity and eternity.

Infinity is not just measureless space, nor is eternity merely endless duration. We humans, constituted as we are, are conscious in an illusory dualistic way. In holistic consciousness, however, we wake up and are released from the strange dream of dualism. We then see that all that seemed real or factual while we functioned in what may be called sense-brain consciousness was indeed a dream, an illusion: imaginative play, as ephemeral as a little child's fantasies. But whereas a child's imaginative play is play, that of adult mankind includes wars, cruelties, stupidities and inhumanities beyond belief. The 'gods' witness it as tragedy; the denizens of hell enjoy it as a comedy. The 'gods' hope to see *homo sapiens* walk the world as a god, immortal. The devils applaud their temporal victory in having reduced man to *homo stultus et criminalis.* But the devils too though they do not know it, will suffer the punishment and salvation of being transmuted into gods through the agency of *homo sapiens,* for in truth I myself am both god and devil. Transcendence contains all and is the All: Totality.

> I am the gambling of the cheat and the splendour of the splendid am I.
>
> (B.G.10.36)

> All-consuming Death and I and the source of all things to come.
>
> (B.G.10.34)

> I am life immortal and also death; being and non-being am I.
>
> (B.G.9.19)

> I form the light and create the darkness; I make peace and create evil: I the Lord do all these things.
>
> (Isaiah 45.7)

> See I have set before thee this day life and good and death and evil:
> I call heaven and earth to record this day against you, that I have set before you life and death, blessing and cursing: therefore choose life, that both thou and thy seed may live.
>
> (Deuteronomy, 30.15.19)

> Now unto eager listeners I will speak of the two spirits created by Mazda.
> They are twins; they reveal themselves as contraries in thought and word and deed, as the Good One (the Holy Spirit) and the Evil One. Together, they make Life and not-life. Thus creation's purpose is fulfilled.
>
> (Ahunavaiti Gatha, Ys. 30.1,3)

In Yasna 19, Zarathushtra asks a question regarding the Creative Word, the *Ahuna Vairya*, which is the most sacred formula of the Zarathushtrians. In his answer, Ahura Mazda mentions in verse 3, 'The beneficent one of my two spirits produced by intoning the Creative Word, the whole rightful creation, which is, and was, and will [continue to] be through the operation of life-promoting action [dedicated] to Mazda.' And in verse 10, 'The nature of this intoning is such that, if the whole material world learned it, it would escape liability to destruction for it would be preserved by reciting it.' The recital must be free from intermission. Verse 15 states: 'The Most Excellent Ahura Mazda proclaimed the *Ahuna Vairya* ; the Most Excellent, the Eternal, caused it to be repeated [after him]. Owing to a pause, evil originated.'

How very significant this is. When we are unoccupied with good thinking, good feeling, good speaking, good doing, when we are *un-conscious* of the Good, whilst we are not holistically conscious, there is a loophole, an enlarging chink in our psycho-physical process through which evil enters and defiles our thinking-feeling-speaking-doing. Constant vigilance is indispensable if we are to live the truly human life. (We have the saying, 'The devil hath work for idle hands'). In another Zarathushtrian scripture, the *Vendidad* (originally the *Vidaevo-datem*, i.e. 'What is given to guard against the demons'), the first of the twenty-two *fargards* (a *fargard* is a section for reciting in a religious ceremony) is an account given by Ahura Mazda to Zarathushtra of how he, through his Holy Spirit, Spenta Mainyu, brought forth all the good creation, and how the hurtful spirit, Angre Mainyu, opposing the Holy Spirit, formed evil things to spoil the good things.

In the *Brihadaranyaka Upanishad* (1.3.1–21) it is said that the *devas* (the gods) and their predecessors the *asuras* (the titans) were the twofold offspring of Prajapati (Lord of Creatures) struggling with each other for the worlds. 'Let us overcome the titans by singing the *Udgitha,*' (i.e. by chanting the *Sama Veda*), said the gods. But the titans rushed in and nullified every attempt by each sense faculty and mind to sing the *Udgitha*. Then the gods called upon prana (the breath of life energy) in the mouth to sing it, and against this, the creative power of the Word, the titans could not prevail but were scattered and perished. Thereafter, the gods were established in comfort and realized the Truth.

Compare this with Plato's *Sophist*, where a stranger from southern Italy who has studied the Eleatic Logic of Parmenides likens the philosophy of his own and earlier times to the mythical battle of the gods and the giants. The confrontation between Idealists and Materialists goes on to this day.

Conditioned as most of us are by the concept of a Creator-God who is all-loving, all-merciful, all-good and all-powerful, we find it very difficult to understand or accept that this God is also the creator of what we, still *in our subhuman stage of development*, call evil. It is not really a case of God creating what we call good and evil but rather *how we react* to any circumstance, event, situation, thing or person. Whatever hurts, displeases or deprives me, I call evil. Conversely, whatever pleases me or promotes and fulfils my ambitions and desires I call good. We have a telling phrase: 'One man's meat is another man's poison.'

The Primordial Creative Energy holds everything within itself in potentiality; the creative process brings forth all that is potential into existence; and thus the Universe manifests. Each and every manifestation is dualistic, for manifestation as a whole functions dualistically: positive-negative, male-female, constructive-destructive, etc. When a war takes place, we say, 'Good!', if the enemy is defeated; but the enemy regards it as a thoroughgoing evil. If the questions in an examination paper suit one particular person, he calls it a 'good' question paper; if they do not suit him because he does not know the answers, it is in his view a 'bad' one. If the interest rates go up, it is 'bad' for borrowers but 'good' for investors. So it is our personal reaction which sets up 'good' and 'evil'.

We react too against natural disasters such as earthquakes, floods, drought, volcanic eruptions, tornados, etc., all of which are part of the living process of the planet. If we are caught up in them, of course we are hurt or destroyed. They are not evil in themselves, though our reaction condemns them as 'evil' because they hurt us or destroy what we have built. It is only good sense to live far away from regions prone to Nature's inclemencies!

Infinity and eternity are to space and time as matter is to mind. As long as I am confined to sense-brain consciousness – analytic, discriminative, separative, dualistic – infinity and eternity are postulates made by the brain. As such they are regarded as opposites to finitude and temporality. For me as I am, space and time and all included in those categories are measurables. When holistic consciousness supervenes, however, infinity and eternity, which are immeasurables, are the 'home' wherein all the limitations imposed by space and time no longer confine my consciousness.

Consider a geometrical point. Strictly speaking, it has no length, no breadth, no depth, no dimensions whatsoever. It is in fact purely conceptual. We are therefore conscious of the pure point as an objective no-thing, though subjectively it is a some-thing. Materially, we can do nothing with this point, but in thought we can.

A countless number of such points, set side by side, will not make a line. But were a point to *move* in any direction in space for a short distance, as if it were endowed with self-motivating life, it would produce a unidimensional line. An infinite number of unidimensional lines placed side by side will not make a square or a rectangle; but if, as in the case of the moving point, a line moves a short distance at any angle to itself, it will produce a two-dimensional surface. This, in turn, moving at right angles to itself, will produce a three-dimensional figure. All these – point, line, surface, three-dimensional figure – are mental pictures only; subjectively real, objectively non-existent.

I, the ordinary man, am conscious through the use of my senses of every single thing that actually exists in the Universe in three-dimensional terms only. My brain cannot *picture* a four-dimensional or multi-dimensional thing, nor can I think that way. The geometry with which we are familiar, in terms of which we can think of and accurately picture anything three-dimensionally, is the 2400-year-old geometry of Euclid. Thus, discursive thinking can raise up a subjectively real world, though it is non-existent objectively. The conceptual framework of this world can nevertheless be as logical and rational as that of the objectively real world of everyday experience.

Now, in the 19th century geometers like Riemann and Lobachevsky produced geometries which broke through the limitations of three dimensions. Whereas space and time had previously been treated as quite separate from each other, Einstein joined them together into a single four-dimensional space-time continuum.

The world of philosophy, and especially of religious philosophy, is also a subjectively real world. Now all the concepts, postulates and conclusions of the objectively real world can be tested by scientific experiment and/or practical experience in daily life. But here too there is a subjective, theoretical component. If my mathematics (the subjective component) is faulty, the objective bridge I build will fall down, or my engine or plane will not move – or, worse still, its failure whilst in movement may kill and/or injure people. The concepts and conclusions of the subjective world of philosophy and religion may and do lead to ethics and ways of life which have to stand the test of experience. If they promote human wellbeing, we preserve them; if not, we have to improve or reject them.

We know that through developments in research techniques we can obtain a fair knowledge of, say, the planet Neptune, which is approximately 2,800 million miles away. That knowledge is all in finite and temporal terms; that is, it is measurable. Even in my restricted state of consciousness, if I think, say or hear the name 'Neptune', Neptune stands at once before my mind's eye. Thought or the spoken word contracts the distance separating me and the planet faster than light, even though the brain that accomplishes this miracle is a material thing. The brain's activity, however, conjures up a picture or knowledge that is structured in and confined to the limited terms of finitude and temporality. Memory of the knowledge of Neptune is at work. 'I' am not in Neptune nor does the planet come to my door! Ordinary consciousness, not holistic consciousness, has been at work.

If in holistic consciousness I turn my attention to Neptune, I do not see or hear or touch the planet or become aware of Neptune and its properties and contents in any manner in which I am aware of everyday life on earth. What actually happens is that I, no longer isolatively and analytically conscious, am one with Neptune. In fact, I *am Neptune* – and Neptune is me! It is not a case of 'I' regarding another object as a separate observer; rather it is a case of 'me' in holistic consciousness *being* Neptune. This 'knowing by being' constitutes one of the apogees of human development. In holistic consciousness you cannot find out the mass, distance, period of rotation or revolution of Neptune: all that has meaning and can be done only in ordinary, everyday consciousness. Clairvoyants might be able to investigate earthly things and properties which are describable in earthly terms – sound, colour, shape, etc. – but holistic consciousness functions in terms which are indescribable.

What then is the use of holistic consciousness?

The question simply does not apply. 'Use' has significance only in the context of finitude and temporality, none in that of the Infinite-Eternal. Meditate on the difference between creation and procreation (see p. 39).

Similarly, there is the difference between our ordinary consciousness and holistic consciousness; and although the latter subsumes the former, the relationship between them cannot be expressed in the language of the finite and temporal. Your well-trained dog can understand and obey your commands, but can it tell another dog the nature of the relationship between you and it?

But there is a difference between the consciousness and expressive ability of a dog and a man. Transcendence is not to be regarded as a separate entity which is conscious holistically. *Transcendence and holistic consciousness are one and the same.* They are the supreme Truth-Wisdom-Love. Writing as a mortal, I have no option but to use words in my attempt to convey – not *convey*, better perhaps *suggest* – to the reader that which is unthinkable and unspeakable. And yet we humans, unlike dogs, possess a degree of sensitivity and impressibility which may help evoke a sympathetic response within the psyche, in which case what is heard or read becomes like a seed which may bear fruit.

By being what you know, that which you know has become part of your self – a more inclusive self than the ordinary self which is isolatively and separatively self-conscious and therefore excludes all that is outside its skin. Self-love characterizes every self. In holistic consciousness, all humanity, even Totality, is embraced; the limited self-love of subhuman consciousness has undergone transmutation into all-embracing Transcendent Love which rejects nothing but endures everything with infinite patience. That is the power which heals and brings everything to fruition.

Thus it is Transcendence Itself, the Unitary Whole, which supervenes through you in holistic consciousness. In India they would call you a Brahmaputra; in Christian terms, a son of God. In India, a perfected holy one declared, 'Aham brahma'smi'. Jesus said, 'I and the Father are One.' Meister Eckhart declared, with special reference to Jesus Christ, 'For man is truly God and God is truly man'. I would unequivocally add to that, 'So it is, potentially, for every person, for it is a fact that there have been perfected holy ones through the centuries.'

In holistic consciousness, your living process is one of ceaseless creative action in eternity and, since your context is infinity, you can 'see the whole world'. Every morning when he woke up, the Buddha looked over the world with the Buddha-eye of compassion and gave help spiritually to those who needed it. But the holistically conscious one never interferes with the fulfilment of the karmic law. Note what Jesus said: 'For verily I say unto you. Till heaven and earth pass, one jot or one tittle shall in no wise pass from the law, till all be fulfilled' (Matt. 5.18); and: 'It is easier for heaven and earth to pass, than one tittle of the law to fail' (Luke, 16.17). St. Paul in his Epistle to the Galatians, (6.7): 'Be not deceived; God is not mocked: for whatsoever man soweth, that shall he also reap.'

The person in whom holistic consciousness supervenes is the lover, teacher and saviour of humanity and of all creation, for what affects one affects all. This supervention charges him or her transcendentally with spiritual energies: Truth, Love, Wisdom, Purity, Goodness, Beauty, Power and Perfection – in such full measure as the organism can healthily absorb. The being of the holy one constantly radiates these energies. Many an ordinary man can sense this emanation and experience an unusual, sublime peace: a harmonizing and healing influence.

Transcendence, by self-limitation, becomes structured. Thus shapeless, formless Transcendence becomes shaped and formed manifestation. Time, as manifested to us, is structured eternity; we are conscious of time; so too infinity and space. So the Immeasurable becomes the measurable to our non-holistic consciousness.

Manifestation is the garment of *our* Origin. The garment of the Truth and Truth Itself are the constantly *beyond*. Like the web spun out of the body (the *being*) of the spider, the manifestation emanates from the Origin, which emanates from Truth: the Infinite-Eternal.

However extensively we approach Truth, it will always be the *beyond* because any and every discovery brings it into the realm of the known, of manifestation, of entity, of the mortal, whereas *It* is immortal and eternal and hence not amenable to discovery by 'me'. 'I' have first to disappear into the ineffable.

Every manifestation, every entity involves limitation or obscuration of the Infinite-Eternal (which Itself nevertheless remains infinite and eternal). Every act of expressing our experience of 'knowing' Transcendence or God is to veil them. All subhuman thought and speech is like a fog obscuring the light of Transcendence; and yet we must nevertheless continue to try to express until the fog is finally dispersed.

When you are in blissful union with Transcendence you do not limit Transcendence, because that blissfulness *in* God is an unknowing 'knowing' of God: a state of union. God is wholly open, utterly naked – and therefore invisible. The very writing, speaking or expounding of Transcendence, of God, however, is sinful in the true sense of the term, for it tries to clothe Transcendence. But strong lovers have to be sinful. . !

We blind mortals cannot see the Transcendent Holy which is completely open, because we are so self-centred. We see only this infinitesimal manifestation called 'I' or 'you', and are totally confined to and absorbed by it.

When I die to 'I', then I am like God, for God is the I that has given up 'I'. But before I can die to 'I', I have to realize 'I' in perfection. My dying to 'I' is truly my sacrifice, my making sacred, my gift to Transcendence – my expiation for shedding my mother's blood at birth. There is also a transcendent reason why I must realize 'I' in perfection. Transcendence is characterized by inexhaustible variety when by self-limitation It creates the infinite particulars of manifestation. Each particular itself embodies a variety: this is its uniqueness. If anyone uncovers this uniqueness, he fulfils one of the purposes of his existence. The genius in any field of art, science, religion or whatever enables Transcendence to fulfil itself transcendentally through that person. Unknowingly but spontaneously and rightly we speak of the 'God-given gift' of that person. When the wise man sees his own uniqueness, he will do all that is necessary to make it shine like a star in the heavens. He lives a dedicated life. He may even succeed in living it sacramentally, as a sacrifice to glorify Transcendence and not for personal vainglory. In this way one realizes the true meaning of individuality at the existential level. The 'I' of mortality is preparing to realize the 'Ehiyeh asher ehiyeh', the 'I Am That I Am' of Transcendence. The ordinary existential being owes it to Transcendence to realize this flowering of his own uniqueness.

What is the relationship between the mortal existent and the immortal Transcendent?

It is this: that the mortal existent is so enriched by the light and power of the Transcendent that there is no pause in creative action in eternity by the Transcendent through him in his perfected state. Therefore, here in the mortal sphere evil can find no place. The Song of Life is not spoilt by any wrong note.

The most discordant note we sound in our life is self-ness. Fully-flowered egohood, true individuality, is unstained by selfness. The particular I am is the microcosmic unitary whole. Consciousness of self as a unitary whole will next realize the Supreme Unitary Wholeness of the One Total Reality: the Universal Individuality which is the Uttermost Indivisibility. You, the unselfed true human, are now holistically conscious. You and your whole living process of thought, word and deed are the concrete manifestation of the heavenly kingdom.

The existential 'you' has attained or achieved nothing. You have successfully reduced your separatively and isolatively conscious self to *no-thing*. You cannot strive to win holistic consciousness for yourself. To do so is to perpetrate the mistake of trying to pluck this sacred fruit of the Tree of Eternal Life. Purify the temple – your own existential being – and Shiva (or the Holy Ghost), the transcendent dweller in the temple, will give you the sacred fruit. You cannot see or hear or touch that dweller, for he becomes you and you become him. And so we say that holistic consciousness supervenes. There is no becoming-process of you or me in this, for all becoming is mortal, whereas holistic consciousness is immortal.

So we cannot *become* the Transcendent; we can only *prepare* ourselves duly to receive It – which is the same as being received by It – by realizing our potential as fully-fledged humans in the true and full sense of the word *human*, meaning 'blissful creator'. So we can see why all procreation, biological and cultural, which is the representation (re-presentation) of Creation by Transcendence, is a truly sacramental activity. Neither by thinking nor by any system of meditation or contemplative prayer in which a hankering self is grasping at a desired (hence preconceived) goal can holistic consciousness be seized or compelled or persuaded to supervene. But if the preparation has been right, and there is pure love (transcendent passion, i.e. an unreserved, unconditional, total surrender of one's whole being to Transcendence, without hoping or expecting anything whatsoever), then, by the grace of Transcendence, it happens. What has to be done has been done. You have made and found ultimate peace with and in God (or Buddha-nature, or Atman. . .):

> That Atman [holistic consciousness] is not this, it is not that (*neti, neti*). It is unseizable, for it is not seized. It is indestructible, for it is not destroyed. It is unattached, for it does not attach itself. It is unbound. It does not tremble. It is not injured.
>
> (Brh. Up. 3.9.26)

> Blessed are the Peacemakers for they shall be called the children of God.
>
> (Matt. 5.9.)

Realizing that peace with and in God means that you, child of man, have relinquished the separate 'I'. In clear consciousness you have died as a being isolated from God. You *are* Transcendence; and henceforth you live as such. Since the existent you is manifest to everyone, you are related to everyone. But no one, unless he himself be gifted with the clear sight of holistic consciousness, can recognize you as such. It took the rending of the veil of the temple, the quaking of the Earth, the darkening of the sun and the rending of the rock, to enable the ordinary subhuman Centurion to say, 'Truly this was the Son of God!'

Today, however, twenty centuries after Jesus Christ, subhumanity is little changed. So the ordinary masses inflict suffering on each other, either willfully or unwittingly, for such is the consequence of being subhuman. You have no option, then, but to give the remainder of your existential life as a ransom for the many. Through you Transcendence may realize (i.e. *makes real*) Its Own transcendence. Bear the agony of the world even unto death. That is how transcendent love emerges, bears fruit, and lives immortally.

And this truly is 'your' immortality, for here 'your' is one with the absolute All, devoid of any separative meaning.

Holistic Consciousness and its Context (continued)

EACH PERSON'S BRAIN, consisting of several billion cells, holds an entire psycho-mental universe. There are also various 'centres': sensitive recipients and transmitters of those archetypal energies which are the modes of functioning of the Primordial Creative Energy. One of the purposes of human existence is to sense these modes and canalize them as beneficent influences in the life of mankind. The holistically conscious human responds sensitively to one or more of them. The particular mode will be the one which is specially characteristic for the individual: for instance, in Zarathushtra's case it was ashoi, purity; in the Buddha's case, prajña, wisdom; in Christ's case, agape, love.

The holy one in meditation, the devotee in contemplative prayer, the yogi in samadhi, is a focal point from which archetypal cosmic energy can radiate in all directions. In ancient times anthropomorphization was unavoidable. The named archangels and angels of the various religions are in fact these cosmic energies. For instance, Michael, he who is like God, is the leader of the heavenly host and is the destroyer of evil. Raphael is the healer and teacher (doctor). Uriel (Auriel) is the illuminator. Gabriel, the strong one of God, the divine messenger announcing resurrection and annunciation and bearing the horn of fertility, is the divine agent of fecundation (on all planes) and personifies the creative power of life – resurrection from death.

There are also energies that are mistakenly called evil or destructive. In fact they are energies which test or 'tempt' you. They are necessary agents for bringing about the transformation of the ill into the well, of the ugly into the beautiful. These helpful and the troublesome energies are not irreconcilables; they are complementaries. It rests with us to be intelligently perceptive in any situation and utilize them sensibly. In silent meditation both categories of energies radiate through the practitioner.

In space-time manifestation, whatever is born will decay and die as its life-energy wanes. Death is lord here. But though matter dies, the incorruptible can resurrect, for Spirit cannot be killed as its life-power is the ceaselessly active energy of the Primordial Creative Energy, and this enables it to manifest over and over in new ways. It is not that spirit is a separate and particular entity reincarnating in different forms. There is only Spirit, not spirits. Spirit being transcendent, is One Alone: the One and Only. You cannot have more than one Transcendent, for then Transcendence would lose its meaning, its actuality. 'My' spirit, 'your' spirit, 'God's' spirit, the 'devil's' spirit is nonsense talk, born of our present limited, befuddled and befuddling consciousness. In holistic consciousness you become well aware of the unitary nature of Spirit, the subtlest form of the Primordial Creative Energy functioning in the context of Infinity-Eternity, and you *see* that Transcendence, by deliberate self-constriction, concretizes Itself *and also* remains as its Whole Unitary Self. The way we ordinarily see, feel and react to death clearly indicates the limited nature of our present consciousness. In holistic consciousness, however, you *see and experience* death as a special technique of change: a transmutative activity leading to perfection, to unimaginable fruition and fulfilment, to immutable truth.

Such it is spiritually – humanly – divinely. In the concretized state of matter, radioactive radium ends up as lead, for material activity is an upside-down spiritual activity: *Demon est Deus Inversus.* Both are precious necessities, however, and so should not be depreciated or discarded. Transcendence Itself takes no sides. We have therefore to learn to be free of preferential choice. It is a question of looking: *just look!* Then you will hold all, support all. If you are a true father or mother, your love will know no exclusiveness. Some of your children will be 'good', some 'naughty'; all your love will flow without interruption to each and every one of them.

At whatever period in history a person's mode of awareness is transformed out of the mortal into the immortal state, his or her psycho-mental functioning – and especially the expression in concept and word of that functioning – is limited to some degree or other. This is due to the prevailing culture, the current climate of thought, which is itself conditioned by the levels of scientific and psychological knowledge maintaining at the particular time. Advancing knowledge in those spheres allows conceptual and verbal expression of ever more profound insights and states of consciousness. Without such knowledge, obscurantism or mystification blight mystical writing.

Mysticism is the heart of religion. In the true mystical experience I meet God. In the religious experience, God meets me in order to see his finite and temporal reflection. That is, God gives himself transcendentally to me by taking up my human-hood into the Godhead. Either way, 'my' humanity is transmuted and invested with godhood. No more am I merely creature; by this metamorphosis I am transformed into the true human – the blissful creator. The mystical experience is the peak point of total self-surrender; the religious, of divine grace.

Ordinarily, a person says 'I am' in order to express his consciousness of his psycho-physical organism. Descartes said, 'Cogito, ergo sum'. But the infinite-eternal Transcendence says, 'Creo, ergo sum'. And since the pure human is inseparably oned with and integrated into Transcendence, he, as whole Transcendence, is infinite-eternal Creator. Those words are 'thoughts' (not hubristic) only insofar as they are symbols (pictures, pointers, indicators) of Transcendent Actuality. Were this not the case, there could not be any such thing as super-sensory experience and phenomena, or miracles, all of which belong to the mortal context and are maya. They are all phenomenal, not immutable; they are effects of certain causes and are in turn causes of further effects. The transcendent Origin alone is absolute. Wonderfully, the whole of changeful maya is changeless Origin displaying Itself.

So all expression of psycho-mental functioning, like

that functioning itself, is limited. We separate the functioning and the expression for a simple reason. When X has a profound insight, he formulates it in thought and/or feeling. When he tries to convey it to Y, his listener or reader, he uses words which have their own specific meaning for him, X, according to his conditioning. But for Y the words have a different meaning according to his own conditioning, even though the difference may be very slight. So the actual content in Y's mind is different from that in X's mind. Different conditioning of the transmitting and of the receiving apparatus, the brains of X and of Y, makes for differences of understanding.

The more science and psychology advance, the easier it becomes for X and Y to bridge the gap created by conditioning. The right and efficient use of knowledge acts like a psychological ascesis. There are also drawbacks associated with the acquisition of knowledge, however, the foremost being the conceit 'I know!'

•

Approach knowledge humbly and cautiously, therefore, constantly keeping an open mind. If, as one grows older, one can honestly declare as Socrates did, 'What I know is that I do not know', then one has become worthy of enlightenment. It is the experience of the wise that even a single profound insight opens up a vista of vast unknown ranges ripe for exploration.

I start loving the knowable. But when 'I know that I do not know', the knowable transforms into the unknown. If you have loved the beloved, especially the 'unsterbliche Geliebte' (the immortal beloved), you will begin to know the beloved. As you and the beloved grow in love, there will come a day when each of you will suddenly realize that you do not know each other. Each of you will discover that the *image* of the other you had in mind was illusory and that the actuality is something transcendent, hence hitherto unknowable. If you continue to grow in love, it becomes transcendental: free of the need or desire for expression – and then you love divinely. In other words, each of you becomes holistically conscious of Transcendent Love and sees that the whole of your previous loving was merely an ephemeral, though happy, play-acting.

Out of the No-thing came I, a no-thing.
Striving to be something, I spun a world of suffering.
Ill, perishing, I saw a spark of light – my nothingness.
Nothingness? Yes, the nothingness of me.
Thereupon No-thing restored no-thing to Itself.
The sight I cannot see is the Pure Vision.
The sound I cannot hear is the Song of Love grown Wise.
Cooled, I know that Love is love at Peace.

No more words, for words can become a meaningless jingle,
a noise, a roaring torrent,
losing me the peace of Being, the bliss of Truth.
Then Beauty hides herself in unbecoming form
and veils herself in careless garb.

Oh for the Formless Unknown, Beloved Unknowable!
For you I must lay my 'me'
In the quenchless flame on your invisible altar.
Grant me your greatest gift,
The extinction of my sense of separate selfhood,
And may Eternity's forgiving mercy
Absolve my sin of separation.
Behold this Passion!
It is also your passion, Creative Power,
And your tireless fiery longing, Immortal Substance!
Your peace is my pain's assuagement.

Raphael! Soma! Heal Substance rent by Desire!

If one can dispel the illusion of separate selfhood, one can walk through the dark portals of death and enter the deathless. This passage can take place in clear consciousness whilst alive in the body.
SEE:

I came into the world possessing nothing,
though being everything,
for, like you,
I am a micro-cosmos.

Though being everything I am nothing,

for each 'I', like each 'you',
is perpetually replaced.

I came all innocent,
wrapped safe in blissful unknowing;
I knew neither pain nor sorrow
nor sickness, nor death.

Then, *they* – parents, relatives, friends –
robbed me of my innocence, my purity,
and plunged me into the darkness of saying 'I',
and of seeing you as 'the other',
and of grasping this or that as 'mine, not yours'.
So were born the twins:
isolative selfhood and separative selfness.

I grew possessive, jealous, envious;
and I knew anger and violence and fear.
I grew lonely.
You, the other, became distant, hostile.

So Love lost. *The sorrow of it!*
For you! For me!
Cain slew his brother Abel, his *alter ego*.
You and I faced opposite ways and walked and walked
– an aeonian walk –
till we met at the very edge of the world;
and at last I saw myself in you
and you saw yourself in me;
and this was journey's end.

And Love rose. Alone. All.
No more you; no more I. Only Us – One.
And the world was pure again. Blessed. Smiling.
And its heartbeat was
the heartbeat of the Cosmos –
Immortality.

•

In loving divinely there is no reciprocity, for reciprocity needs two who are separate. When duality disappears, holistic consciousness prevails and the illusion of otherness vanishes. In holistic consciousness, therefore, love makes no demands whatsoever. Being transcendent, it is eternal, infinite. Like the sun which cannot stop ceaselessly and indiscriminately shining and radiating light and heat, transcendent love shines and radiates choicelessly from the one in whom holistic consciousness supervenes. Such is God's love. And just as we open an umbrella to shade ourselves from the sun, so too all of us who are ignorant and unskilled interpose the thick black cloud of separative selfness against the healing love of Transcendence.

In duality-bound love, dependent upon reciprocity, we subhumans are subject to alternating love-hate: to possessiveness, which entails jealousy, suspicion and violence. There is expectation and demand according to our conditioning; fidelity, freedom and trust are conditional. The true joy of love is therefore a vain dream; and many a child is a lust child, perhaps conceived under the influence of intoxicants, and not a truly wanted love-child. True love-children can be saints like Satyakama Jabala or geniuses like Leonardo da Vinci.

In divine loving there is death and creation. This death is neither loss nor annihilation. It is a newness so new that nothing that ever was or will be can be like this immediate present. It is not re-cognizable. It is a change so great that it is beyond man's comprehension. Such fruitive dying or creative death bears the hall-mark of true creation – new and yet immutable – for it involves the destruction (again, not annihilation but transmutation) of the immediate *is*.

Eternal Living is a constant dying through love.

Even in our ordinary daily life, starting from the very instant of conception in the mother's womb, the ceaseless change of the body's growth is actually a dying out of the state prevailing at one instant to be reborn in the new state prevailing at the next. This goes on until the body reaches – sweetly and happily? – its final end, its Sabbath. What happens between conception and Sabbath is our personal responsibility: dutifully to work out the purpose(s) of our existence (our 'standing out of' the Infinite-Eternal). So indeed love is inextricably interwoven with death and creation.

Until holistic consciousness supervenes, all our concepts and words, even those insights which seem to have touched profound depths, are confined to the finite and mortal. We are limited beings. As such, since the finite can never contain the infinite, Absolute Truth is always the *beyond* for any psycho-physical being, always the unpenetrated, even by perfected holy ones.

Existence, which is manifestation, means 'that which stands out of'. Out of what does it stand? It stands out of the Absolute, out of that which the manifested can never reach, never become, never realize. (The root of the word 'real' is the Latin *res:* 'a thing'). Even spirit, the subtlest counterpart of matter, is manifestation; whatever can be experienced or thought of and spoken of is manifestation. Although the perfected holy one is the child of God, it is God that subsumes the child, never the other way round.

The absoluteness of the Absolute can never be un-absolutized. Therefore I – the child, the perfected holy one, the manifested God, the peacemaker – must de-manifest so that God Alone is God, Truth Alone is Truth. But no one's divine dissolution means annihilation. Transcendence, as embodied in you or me or anything manifested, is never, can never, be annihilated. It rests in its eternal home after its cosmic journey through any and every universe, through the totality of its creative action.

What happens is something like this:

You and I are sitting in this room. When we walk out of it, the room remains the same room. Transcendence is the infinite-eternal room, all-holding and all-emptying. It is also all-absorbing. The room in which we sat together, meditated or prayed or loved together has our 'atmosphere', our 'influence' left in it when we leave. If a clairvoyant or psychically sensitive person enters that room, he or she can sense or 'read' that atmosphere.

When death effects my de-manifestation, Transcendence as Totality takes in all the effects of my life's activity in terms of thought, word and deed. *Totality reaps* all that I have sowed. If what I sowed was true and complete fulfilment of the purpose(s) of Transcendence through me, all is well. Wholly absorbed in Transcendence, isolatively and separatively self-conscious 'I' ceases entirely. But if my sowing failed to fulfil its purpose(s), Totality expresses another existential being, a *new* mortal, *not* 'me' reincarnated, till the particular purpose of Transcendence is realized. Projecting this on the global scale, might we not tentatively suggest that the current population explosion is a measure of mankind's previous failures to fulfil the purpose of Totality?

The idea of innumerable incarnations climaxing in Nirvana or moksha (liberation – but that is always only here and now) or of a single life climaxing in an eternal heaven or hell (it is in fact logically impossible for a limited being to produce an unlimited consequence), brings *me* to an abrupt full stop; but in the Infinite-Eternal there is no full stop.

Man asks, 'Why did God. . . .?' – and the immediate answer is, 'Be quiet, be silent. God knows, Transcendence knows'.

And this can only be so, for God's 'knowledge' entirely passes manifestation's understanding. *I* do not know; *you* do not know; neither you nor I will ever know. So we can only be content to find out how we can prepare ourselves to be received by Transcendence, our Origin. And remember that our origin is a manifestation of Origin. We, as we are at present, are simply the bricklayers, not the architect. Whoever sees this wholly will be freed of self-misunderstanding and of his actual selfness. We cannot strive to achieve selflessness as a goal, for any goal preconceived by us whilst we are still blinded by our selfish state will always be misconceived. But note how the healthy growth of a newborn baby simply *happens*. It can never be prefigured by anybody. Life, that wonderful mystery, grows the child. So too with spiritual realization: we can only assist or hinder life's alchemy.

When holistic consciousness supervenes, you the dewdrop have met the shining sea. In fact you *are* now that shining sea, for in the context of infinity and eternity, the immeasurables, you or I have ceased to be measurable, separate parts of a composite Totality. You or I, integrated into the Whole, are no longer separate 'existents'. We *are* the Whole Totality. This is Transcendental Death, which is identical with Life Eternal. This integrated wholeness is the actuality of love.

Love, transcendentally, is identical with Primordial Creative Energy, with Creativity. Genesis, 1.26 may well be understood in this way: 'And Elohim *minded*, Let us create Man [i.e. archetypal man] in our own living likeness'. Thus archetypal man is imbued with divine potentiality: divinity lies latent, sleeping within him. One of the great purposes of his existence is, through love, to let the sleeping (the temporarily forgotten) divinity awaken, grow into full self-realization and, liberated as the fully perfected and hence holy *hu-man*, function freely in terms of holistic consciousness. All this is Transcendent Love in creative activity in eternity, spiritually, and also in organic manifestation, materially.

Psycho-physical man, the organism, having evolved from a primate and being constituted of matter, suffers all the limitations incident upon materiality. Matter came into being through the concretizing of pure Primordial Creative Energy and the concomitant constricting of Pure Consciousness, which consequently evolved a humanity possessed of a materially conscious mind oblivious of its divine origins. But matter itself is Transcendence self-restricted so that Transcendence Itself may ultimately realize and be fully conscious of Its own Transcendent being, Nature and Powers through the perfected human who has remembered his latent divinity and released it into its original splendour. The Zen Buddhist phrase is to 'see the Original Face'. Let man see, really *see*, what wonders love can do. In a very curious way, then, man is instrumental in redeeming and liberating Transcendence through Transcendence.

Love for anyone or anything is true, total and perfect when there is perfect love for the Unitary Whole, which means love for every one and every thing. Charity, the giving of gifts and so forth, has to be like the flower that wafts its perfume onto the air without caring who or what receives it. Whoever receives the delightful fragrance, however, will be blissfully aware of the receiving. In this way a gift is truly divine.

As said above, Love is identical with the Primordial Creative Energy. It is *our* Origin, which cannot be located anywhere, nor has It anything to do with time, for Its context is infinity and eternity. The Origin is a mystery, as unknowable as Absolute or Pure Consciousness. Wipe out all these words and concepts and you have Origin – but at the same time, Origin is that which called for these words and concepts.

As it concretizes Itself, Origin forgets Itself almost completely. So it is in the most concrete matter, that pin-point state of fundamental substance which explodes with such vast violence at the Big Bang that reduces primordial order to a primordial chaos of subatomic particles and creates space and time. Transcendent Love and procreative love display wonderful similarities as well as differences. The involutionary outgoing path climaxes in explosive violence; the return path climaxes in the restoration of perfect order and transcendent peace, neither being inertly static nor restlessly dynamic but blissfully creative. On the return path Origin remembers Itself through and in man. This is remembrance: the anamnesis of the Christian, the zikr of the Sufi, the smriti of the Hindu yogi, mukta or mahatma – growing in humanity and culminating as the fully-fledged human.

Each one of us can be a flash of awakening as we remember Origin in full consciousness. Man is indispensable to God and God is the inner light ever shining in our darkness. To say this is the same as saying that the God that is veiled in manifestation is indispensable for revealing God to God. It all happens if we care totally for Absolute Truth, with that perfect love which is at once death and creation.

•

The popular saying, 'There is nothing new under the sun', holds good to a certain extent in the finite and temporal context to which our analytical discriminative consciousness – the Buddhists call it viññana – is confined. But everything is new under and over the sun in the transcendent context of the Infinite-Eternal. The usual conceptions of infinity, eternity and immortality are rather static and uncreative. They are negated in holistic consciousness as and when it functions in its transcendent mode.

Eternity is the actuality. Constituted as we are, we are confined in our viññana mode of awareness to linear time: to past, present and future. In ancient India the division and range of time was as follows according to Bhaskara's *Surya Siddhanta and Siddhanta Shiromani*:

> 100 Trutis made 1 Par; 30 Pars, 1 Nimesh; 10 Nimeshas, 1 Kashtha; 30 Kashthas, 1 Kala; 30 Kalas, 1 Ghatika; 2 Ghatikas, 1 Kshana; 30 Kshanas, 1 day

> and night. The solar system lasts for a long time – $10^{19} \times 2,239,488$ Years.

In the Buddhist system of the *Mahavibhasa*, the *Abhidharmakosha* and the *Loka Prajñapti*:

> 1 Ksana (the smallest unit of time) is 1/90th part of the duration of a thought; 120 Ksanas made 1 Tatksana; 60 Tatksanas, 1 Lava; 30 Lavas, 1 Muhurta (48 minutes); 5 Muhurtas, 1 Kala (Buddhist hour); 6 Kalas, 1 Day (24 hours). The Buddhists had the month and year and larger units called *yugas, kalpas,* and the largest, the *mahakalpa* which was the measure of the life-cycle of the world.

The Jains believe that a man has 8,400,000 incarnations before he realizes Nirvana. Assuming an average of 25 years for each life and that rebirth takes place immediately after death, the world would have to survive at least 210 million years.

The Zarathushtrians classically thought in terms of a 12,000-year cycle. Contrast with the above, modern Western computations. At the lower end of the scale science has talked of 10^{-15}, 10^{-21}, 10^{-23} of a second; and theoretically of 10^{-35} and of 10^{-43} of a second when the curtain rolled up on the cosmic stage with a Big Bang around 15 billion years ago. The Universe is an expanding Universe at present and if it continues to expand through all time it will become cooler and less dense. Stars will burn out and become dark remnants through gravitational collapse. In about 10^{30} years most of the Universe will consist of 'black holes' i.e. bodies so dense that no light can escape from them, hence invisible. But even black holes emit a trickle of radiation and a few elementary particles. The matter and energy trapped in the hole 'tunnels' out, so that each object in the Universe becomes a perfect sphere in about 10^{65} years. Tunnelling will destroy the black holes; most matter will be converted into radioactive energy only to be dissipated by the expansion of the Universe, leaving only dead stars and planets. Through radioactive decay or fusion, all objects will become solid iron after about $10^{1,000}$ to $10^{2,000}$ years. Nothing will happen after this until the remains may get compressed into a black hole by a quantum mechanical process which would require quite a long period of time. The number of zeros required to express this period in years is 10^{77}.

Each black hole will evaporate into radiation through tunnelling. Thus all matter will ultimately radiate away and the Universe will become no-thing. Time then comes to its end; absolute silence reigns – so say some modern scientists. In former times, however, people in Asia preferring 'to be' rather than 'not to be' declared that the R.I.P. phase of the Universe would be as long as its manifesting phase – and that the whole performance would repeat itself again and again.

What are we to make of all this? I for one do not know. It may well, be asked,'How can we put a measure on the immeasurable – on eternity?' But it is interesting to note that both the ancient East and the modern West have considered time on the minute scale – and also on the vast scale.

•

We have said above that the Truth is always *beyond*. Truth, however, embraces no grades of truthfulness: Truth is Truth, absolutely. But grades of understanding and perception mark the extent of *our realization* of Truth. The culmination of these grades is expressed by the person who realizes in his own unique way. Although unique, the verbal expression is often similar, sometimes the same.

For instance, Jesus said,'I am the way, the truth and the life', and 'I and the Father are one' (John 14. 16 and John 10. 30). The Upanishadic sages affirmed, 'Aham brahma'smi', I am Brahman. Shri Krishna: 'I am the Path' (B.G. 9. 18), 'the Truth' (B.G. 10. 4). The Buddha realized and taught the Four Noble Truths and the Noble Eightfold Way to Nirvana, which is the cessation of all greed, hatred and delusion. And the Upanishads affirmed the identity of Brahman and Atman. The Sufi mystic Al-Hallaj meanwhile affirmed at his crucifixion 'Ana'l haqq': 'I am the Creative Truth'.

Such statements express a unique realization of Truth by a unique being. Neither the being, the realization nor its verbal expression is higher or nearer Truth than any other being and his realization. Each is complete, whole, perfect. This is one of the significant implications of uniqueness. We see especially in the cultural sphere the absurdity of comparison; this composer or artist is superior to that one. We lay down fixed criteria for making such discriminative statements, which only express our preferential choice or reaction, indicating our conditioning or natural bent. When we encounter this in the sphere of religion the consequences are often troublesome, sometimes disastrous and inhuman and, in the case of militant evangelism, unwise.

The holistically conscious human is free of comparison and competition. In the Transcendent Context of infinity and eternity where there is no duality or multiplicity, higher-lower, superior-inferior, gain-loss, equality– inequality, self-not self, success-failure, etc., have no meaning. Very significant is the fact that those perfected holy ones around whose names great religions have arisen, and those other holy ones whose names are unknown but who gave supreme teachings regarding the living of the holy life, refrained from producing reasoned philosophical systems, knowing that such systems are not The Truth, because all assumptions made in the mortal context of the finite and temporal are only pale shadows of the functioning of holistic consciousness in the Infinite-Eternal context: mere evanescent visions born of a transient flash of Transcendence.

The great holy ones who were past all sorrow, free of all evil, were Truth embodied. When you are the Truth, you need no instruction, no argument, no conceptual-verbal system to help or enable you to see the Truth. You cannot avoid seeing every one and every thing truly. You are not liable to delusion. You dispel all illusions even as the risen sun dries up the morning dew. Each of the holy ones, being a fully-fledged human, lived his life as a perfect example for his own particular time, circumstance and society. After his death intellectuals indulged in debate, sometimes wasteful, sometimes profitable hermeneutically.

Scholars naturally and justifiably see an implied metaphysic or an ontology hidden in spiritual teachings – as for instance, the Samkhya philosophy in the teachings of the Buddha. The founder of a tradition teaches a way of life culminating in the realization of the *summum bonum* towards which the neophyte aspires. The teaching must naturally be comprehensible to those taught. The teacher's medium of communication, apart from his personal living of the teaching, is unavoidably the written and the spoken word, which inevitably involves a metaphysic or ontology. Even though it may not be actually enunciated by the teacher, it exercises an influence upon the subsequent formulation or systematization of his teachings by his followers.

Most of the great spiritual teachers of the past affirmed Transcendence in Its theistic mode: the Judaic Jehovah, the Zarathushtrian Ahura-Mazda, the Christian God the Father, the person of Vishnu in Vaishnavism and of Shiva in Shaivism, the Allah of the Islamic peoples, the Satya (Eternal Truth) or Akal Purusha of the Sikhs. The Upanishadic non-theistic form is Brahman, and also Parabrahman (Shri Krishna's 'the origin of the Father', Pitamaha – B.G. 9. 17).

The Buddha chose a non-theistic formulation, affirming Transcendence as 'the unborn, unbecome, unmade, uncompounded'. Orthodox Buddhism trenchantly rejects the Hindu atman. The Buddha's analysis includes discriminitive consciousness, viññana, as one of the five constituents or khandhas composing the manifested person. Viññana is, like the other four khandhas, perishable. But the Buddha also uses the phrase 'viññanam anidassanam anantam sabbato pabham' – 'consciousness which is characterless, unending [and therefore without beginning], everywhere shining' – in at least two places: (1) in the 49th discourse of the *Majjhima Nikaya*, in which the Buddha addresses Baka the Brahma (the phrase can also be translated as 'consciousness which cannot be characterised, which is lucid in every respect' in this context); and (2) in the eleventh discourse of the *Digha Nikaya*, where the person addressed is Kevaddha and where the word 'paham' (meaning 'accessible') is used instead of 'pabham'. Clearly this phrase is the Buddha's equivalent of the Upanishadic atman, which is repeatedly presented in negative form as birthless, deathless, uncharacterisable; as 'neti, neti' ('not this, not that').

The aphoristic form in which the teachers couched most of their teachings has the great advantage of brevity. When, however, brevity is compressed to its extreme limit it can become unintelligible – as in the classic case of Badarayana's *Brahma Sutras*.

The great and authentic spiritual teachers, possessed of clear understanding of the state of subhumanity, of its sorrow and the frustration of the purpose(s) of existence, were primarily concerned with healing and enlightening man: with man's permanent wellbeing and happiness. They had realized the peace and bliss of perfect human fulfilment in their own persons and, as a result, being embodiments of compassions and wisdom, spent their lives in showing the way to all those who genuinely longed for liberation from all that shackled them to ignorance and sorrow. This concern derived from their transcendent love for all that lives without exception. Transcendent love has no vested interest whatsoever.

The conventional theist may ask,'Why is love for God not mentioned?' The honest and unequivocal answer is, 'First become able to smile with your whole heart at all that lives, then you will know exactly what "Love of God" is. Also, you will always ask the right question.'

The holy ones saw that the root of all suffering is man's un-holistic, isolative and separative self-consciousness. So the main part of their teaching was directed to showing how to live daily life in such a manner as to transform fragmentary self-consciousness into holistic consciousness. They knew in fact that it is the manner or mode in which a man is conscious of himself and his world which determines whether he will live a pure life or an evil life.

•

How does one live so that holistic consciousness may supervene?

The method for producing a desired result is always sought. That is perfectly right in the worlds of science, mechanics, economics, politics, sociology – in short, in the world of the finite and temporal, of techniques and limitation. It is, however, wrong with respect to the Infinite-Eternal.

The question might quite probably be asked simply out of intellectual curiosity; or the questioner may be cynical or incredulous; he may indeed not be entirely serious. Even if he is genuinely interested, he is actually asking, 'How must *I* live so that holistic consciousness may supervene through *me*?' Note that the question is self-oriented. Any self-orientation is an attempted sundering of the Unitary Whole and in consequence must invariably spell defeat.

Furthermore, if I say, 'I only want to be with God', my wanting is always associated with the belief, 'I shall know I am one with God when the union takes place'. Here we have duality again – I and God. 'I' do not see that only when my desire is extinct is God's Will fulfilled. No-one can compel God; it is God who takes a person up unto Himself.

But I, the self-conscious person, can only start with my desire. If, however, it intensifies into pure longing for Transcendence (the tadvanum of the Upanishads) and my self-surrender becomes total, the baptism by fire takes place. *My* desire then burns away, the isolativeness of self-consciousness disappears and 'Thy Will O Lord, not mine' supervenes. Finally, the Infinite-Eternal completely subsumes me and in that perfect union there is only God, only Transcendence.

So I as a finite and mortal entity can only offer myself to Transcendence as an unconditional sacrifice. What is offered has to be pure; then there is no obstruction to the free functioning of God's Will, which *creates*, unlike man's desire, which only *procreates*.

So we see that the question, 'How must I live so that holistic consciousness supervenes through me?', is a wrong question with respect to the Infinite-Eternal.

Have you never experienced that transcendental union with Nature or with another person in which not a vestige of separate self-consciousness remained? When there was no sense of 'I' and the beloved as separate entities? When even the intensest consciousness of 'us' was transcended, the brain was quite silent and only the fact of unitary wholeness was there? And only some time after the divine event you became aware of the ineffable bliss of the holy union, the wholeness?

No? Then you have never known the perfection of love, spiritual and organic.

Yes? Then you have realised Transcendent Love and have understood the total disappearance of separate

self-consciousness in your one-ness in God. Holistic consciousness has supervened.
Do not make the mistake of saying, 'I must get rid of the ego'. Do you get rid of yourself when you are in union with your beloved? Not at all. You are the Universal Self then. 'You' are, just as 'I' am, the apparatus, the objective means by which Transcendence concretely manifests and thereby realizes its own transcendence as the perfect human. This apparatus is not a mechanical contrivance or a scientific machine. It is a living means. Have you not heard the term, 'the Living God'?

Let us return to the question. 'In what manner must you or I live so that Holistic Consciousness may supervene?'

I do not know the way for you. Being unique, you have to discover and try out the way for yourself, keeping the mind flexible and open. Sayings like 'Following in the footprints of the master' are impracticable. Since each one of us is unique, no one's feet will fit into the footprints of any master. Moreover, each one being himself, he cannot see and understand precisely how the master saw and understood the Truth.

Nevertheless, although you and I are different from each other by virtue of uniqueness, there is also a general sameness by virtue of basic structure. All human bodies – bones, blood, organs, limbs, etc. – are very similar; so too the way in which the organs function. We all feel pleasure and pain, have similar reactions bodily and psychically, and the same basic needs – food, shelter and warmth – even though the extent of those needs may differ widely. But whilst our bodily psychical *reactions* may be similar, our upbringing and education, heredity and environment, and our own individual circumstances may be such that our emotional and intellectual *responses* and the sensitivity, refinement and intensity of our consciousness and perceptivity may be quite different. They may be poles apart.

It is necessary to understand the difference between reaction and response, because the discovery of one's individual way is intimately involved in it. To understand this let us first consider how our basic conditioning gives rise to similar reactions. This basic conditioning is like a psychological counterpart of the bodily skeleton.

A mother suckles her newborn infant, who is happy

as long as he is given the breast. If she thinks he has had enough and takes him off prematurely, he protests and may even fly into a tantrum. Right from birth the human creature reacts angrily against the stoppage of pleasure! Hate and its brood – anger, dislike, enmity, violence – are born of frustrated pleasure. Whoever gives pleasure is loved; whatever thwarts pleasure is hated or at least disliked. As the child grows up, self-consciousness as a separate, isolative being intensifies.

'I like', 'I wish', 'I want', 'I must have or take' become dominant. Greed and self-orientation are at the root of most unwholesomeness. But the child does not know this for at this stage he is at the mercy of his natural urges and his philosophy of life is summed up in one word: *pleasure*. At the same time the youngster is exhorted to be good, which mainly means to do what his elders want him to do. It is believed that happiness lies in this direction. He may receive a reward for compliance or punishment for disobedience. He may be taught simple virtues: to speak the truth, not hurt but help younger members of the family and pets, refrain from taking other peoples' belongings without permission, not to swear or use harsh language, to observe the appropriate courtesies, to deal honestly and with fair play towards equals and elders – thereby sowing the seeds for cooperation and even altruism in later life.

Training by parents and teachers is directed towards preparing the young person to earn his or her own living, to succeed professionally in a competitive world, to fulfil ambitions and generally 'enjoy' life. Ignorant of true happiness, people are always talking and struggling to 'enjoy' life! The pleasure drive is an all-powerful urge, but what is not taught – partly because it cannot be taught by another person although it can certainly be learnt by anyone who cares – is self-understanding, the purpose(s) of one's personal existence, one's true place in the scheme of things and how to flower into full human-ness.

Here, the whole question and influence of morality and virtue, self-discipline (not self-'control' as ordinarily understood, for that is usually repression), the release of intelligence and the spontaneous and natural expression of one's uniqueness all come into play; also true religiousness. The last is not indulgence in the postures of piety or the mouthing of mere beliefs, doctrines and dogmas of conventional religious teaching. It lies in seeing Truth for and by oneself and living by it, as the great spiritual teachers of the past did. You *have* to see for yourself, just as you have to breathe for yourself. Others may help a little, but enlightenment and fulfilment come only from within yourself. Also never try to copy any master, however great and holy. You may succeed – but only in being a caricature, which would not confer much credit on the master.

The indispensable foundation of the good life is virtue. The forms of conventional morality – which include so-called good manners – are usually presented to us by our elders as living according to the accepted traditions of our family, society, race and religion. At the start they may be a genuine expression from the heart by one person to another and can give rise to friendly relationship. In time however, they can become hollow shams: things that 'must be done' in the interests of social respectability and acceptability. Genuine good feeling gradually fades then and the observed manners degrade into pretence and hypocrisy. Some are downright cruel and unjust. Think of countries where it is good form that a faithful wife immolate herself on her late husband's funeral pyre; where women have a lower status than men and must necessarily be content with a lower salary or an inferior position. Think too of the tradition in at least one part of the world where it is bad manners *not* to burp after dinner as a sign of grateful appreciation to your host!

So look askance at all traditions; but, to be fair, first consider all traditions with nice discrimination. All 'good manners' are traditions; and many a tradition is good and its continuance is desirable as long as the genuine good feeling of the heart animates it. It is traditional good manners to keep your word on the personal level and, on the international one, to observe treaty commitments. See what happens when such treaties are torn up – disaster. Masses of people react in similar ways due to their upbringing and education.

Pointers for living the virtuous life are found in the great religions: for instance, the Ten Commandments of Judaism and the Triad of Good Deed, Good Word and Good Thought of Zarathushtrianism. In Buddhism there are the Pancha Sila or Five Precepts.

Transcendent Love is the root of all virtue. Jesus said: 'This is my commandment [entolé = 'things given in charge']: Love one another, as I have loved you. There is no greater love than this, that a man should lay down his life for his friends' (John 15. 12. 13). And the Buddha taught (D. 3. 187): 'The friend who is sound of heart lays down even his life for your sake', and:

> Who proves a comrade in your hour of need,
> Him may ye rightly call a friend indeed.
>
> (D. 3. 184)

Love is the harmonious expression of our psycho-physical energy promoting health, happiness and peace. It starts in infancy as attachment to who or whatever gives sensational pleasure; in childhood to whoever satisfies desire. Parents and playmates are consequently the earliest loved ones, though the former are also feared for they can frustrate desires and inflict sanctions.

In adolescence, Nature, concerned with the preservation of the human species, introduces a new element in the growing youngster: sexual desire, which remains a dominant passion for the greater part of the physically matured person's life. 'Falling in love' gives rise to many qualities: tenderness, caring, desire to please the loved one in as many ways as possible (even at a cost to oneself); but also less lofty impulses, such as to possess and enjoy the loved one for oneself exclusively, and to persuade or bend the other to one's own will, etc.

In relation to all outside the family circle, you cannot love to order or try to love. Likes and dislikes, attractions and aversions take place naturally, inexplicably. You can attribute them to your genes or blame your 'daimon', as you please; but to *try* to love usually ends in failure, for love is not something to be achieved. It arises spontaneously and grows naturally – and then it is magic. All mental searching for a cause or explanation is silenced: you are at one with a mystery. You can nourish this tender flower and let its beauty be the guiding star of your life, or, as unfortunately happens time and again, destroy it and make (and suffer) hell.

The world thinks of love between the sexes in terms of sexual possession and expression. Ascetic philosophies consider sexual expression to be the greatest obstacle to spiritual fulfilment. That is so when one becomes the abject slave of the pleasure drive and sexual love degrades into lust – which, unhappily, is not too difficult. Consequently the Buddha repeatedly and sternly warned his monks and disciples against the perils of the senses and especially against the lure of women. So did other monastic orders as well as many of the great philosophers. Plato went so far as to dub the feminine principle as the principle of evil – what might his mother, Perictione, have said to that?, one wonders.

Man and wife are not just any man and any woman but two people who have given themselves wholly to each other for a life-long relationship of united being and living. When harmony exists between such a man and wife, sexual expression is one of the profoundest expressions of love. The act of marital congress has also to become a sacramental art. There are times when man and wife can both be in a state of deep longing that is not just psychical turmoil. When the strong, gentle wave of bodily desire rises undemandingly but with sweet compulsion to its height, let the artistry of Eros have skilful play with the body in the sacred act of love.

Now, there are hints in some scattered scriptural writings that each partner should bring to mind the activity and purpose of the life-urge. Life is sacred, possessed of a motivation and power betstowed upon matter by Transcendence. Born of evolution, it is an influence to restore in us the memory of our Origin – hence its sanctity – which was forgotten during the involutionary plunge into matter. Think of Nature's prodigality with seed in the plant, animal and human kingdoms. This prodigality is the organic material counterpart to the transcendental infinite creativity of Transcendence. Plant and animal expend seed out of ignorance; they do not know why it happens that way; all they know is pleasure. So too with subhumanity; but intelligent, awakened humans can plant and receive seed sacramentally.

Remain intensely aware of complete unity with all manifestation, materially and psychically, throughout love-making, offering it as a sacrificial gift to all existence. Let the whole meditative experience reach its natural climax, preserving the spirit of sacrifice (making sacred) right to the end. You may then procreate one of those rare humans who flower into perfected holy ones: the finest fruits of humanity. Both man and wife must live the true religious life before this can be realized, however. Treat the whole topic with utmost reverence – or else you may reap much sorrow.

Understanding this, we can perhaps sense a meaning in the story that Abraham, aged 100 years and his wife Sarah, aged 99, gave birth to Isaac (the name means 'Laughter'). Ordinarily the newborn child whimpers or cries. The legendary account of Zarathushtra's birth states that he laughed when he was born – an Iranian Isaac! Can we see a meaning too perhaps in the Greek, Indian and Norse myths of Zeus or Apollo, Indra or Shiva, Wotan or any gods or godesses, fathering or mothering heroes and saints etc? Gods and godesses, devas and devis represent human beings gifted with special qualities or powers. Who knows what was the state of consciousness or what was in the minds of those couples whose procreative love-making gave birth to miraculous offspring? All the pantheons present human psychology, powers and qualities in apotheosis; our procreative power is therefore a re-presentation in our limited human terms of the unlimited creative power (the Zarathushtrian kshathra) of Transcendence.

We must note carefully that in the procreative act the sense of touch plays the paramount part. Like the 'touch' of Transcendence which lifts our consciousness into the holy state, our physical sense of touch can evoke holistic consciousness, if only momentarily. So can the other senses if used purely and skilfully in the appropriate way. Take the person who steps out of the front door of his lonely country cottage in Dorset on a frosty winter's night and sees the entire sky down to the horizon filled with brilliantly glittering stars; or the one who in mid-summer looks out of his tent in Kashmir and is spellbound by snow-clad Himalayan peaks bathed in moonlight. As has happened to the writer on a few exceptional occasions, he will simply exclaim, 'God!', in sheer wonder. But the sound of his voice will be a faint echo of the voice of the Infinite-Eternal proclaiming Truth. One is transformed by such immensity, though it is only a momentary flash transmuting a worldly consciousness of beauty into a holistic vision of Transcendence. But what a moment! – embodying infinity and eternity!

Thus one learns a great lesson: the senses are *not* to be despised, for they are man's distinctive and indispensable assets. Truly human living, however, requires their right use.

In chapter 5 the development of the conflict between reason and revelation and the rise to dominance of the masculine rational principle and of experimental science were outlined. In our 20th century, science and psychology have initiated the reinstatement of the intuitive, aesthetic and emotional feminine principle, by which there is immediate apprehension. Revelation, direct seeing, is akin to this principle, but its proper conceptual and verbal expression needs the correct and effective use of the rational, formal, scientific and mathematical principle.

Whilst the vigilance centre in the brain is not in need of sleep, man's sense organs and brain carry on the business of daily living. He is awake, receptive. On the one hand, the sense impressions are responsible for his attachments and aversions, his bondage. On the other hand, if he exercises discernment, the senses are the means of his freedom and fulfilment, for they are the instruments of that close observation that allows and enables holistic consciousness to supervene.

Holistic consciousness supervenes quietly in a natural, mysterious and silent manner similar to that in which life grows the organism. The secret lies in ceasing to be a noise-maker intruding upon the cosmos and upon oneself. Speaking positively, be the *silent watcher*.

So let the senses function freely. Look, listen, touch, taste and smell, observing with as full attention as possible. At first, reactions for or against what you observe *will* arise within; and the brain *will* talk back all the time, saying: 'That is right . . . I don't agree . . . That is new to me . . . How absurd . . .! What a bore . . .!, etc., etc. – ad infinitum. Keep observing as patiently and dispassionately as possible, not like a tourist who wants to see a whole continent in a week! Reject nothing, accept nothing, condemn nothing, approve nothing. In this way you will see the fact as the fact and understand how it comes into being, how it changes and what are its consequences.

Similarly, the total factual observation of your brain talking back at your sense impressions will reveal to you exactly what you are. You will then understand yourself thoroughly and also understand what any person who is talking or working with you is like inwardly.

In due time you will find that the brain's reactive chatter will calm down. Finally, it will stop and the calm and clarity of the inner silence will enlighten you. In the ancient school of Pythagoras, freshmen spent their first two years as akoustikoi, listeners, just as sravana, listening, was the first stage of learning for the pupils of the Upanishadic teachers. It is a most arduous discipline, but if you care for Truth above all else such pure, bare observation will tell you the truth of all things as they are. This means that you become clearly conscious of that which you observe. You are then on the way to knowing by being what you observe. In the process all the beliefs, convictions, anxieties and fears characterizing your worldly state of consciousness will disappear. You will know the Truth – and 'the Truth will make you free' (John 8. 32). The psyche, emptied of all clutter, will be filled with the knowledge which is Truth, and you who are belief-empty will be faith-full. Unknown to you, Pure Mind, functioning freely through your empty psyche (the clean temple) will release a constantly self-replenishing spiritual energy which will enable you to be a still, silent observer, just as Transcendence attentively observes the entire cosmos.

Now holistic consciousness supervenes. This is the pure meditative state. *Meditation is creative action in eternity*. The purified and pacified senses are the cords of communion with and in Transcendence. At-oned with Totality, you can unerringly make the right response to whatever comes to you. The ineffective noise of mere re-action no longer disturbs you and your environment, for in this still and silent state you accept the Universe transcendentally, without being bound in any way by that acceptance. This cannot happen by thinking or by prayer or by any *laid down system of meditation – which is mere verbal ritual*. The activity of the discursive mind, the wheel of imagination (image-making) has to be completely stilled before the transcendental Silence can prevail. It happens through the senses, not by thought, for the rationality and logicality of thought split the wholeness (the holiness) of Truth. When looking or listening reaches its most intense and perfect apogee, all naming, analysing, dissecting, describing, categorizing and comparing comes to its rest. No longer is the seen or the heard plucked out of the Universe. No longer is the Universe (etymologically 'That which is turned into a unity', from the Latin *unus*, 'one', and *vertere*, 'to turn') wounded by mankind's despoiling and divisive activites.

Why must the activity of the discursive mind be stilled? Because every symbol, expression, thought or word belongs to the realm of the finite and temporal, the mortal. The Still Silence, however, is the immortal Origin. The Buddha called this still state *nirodha* (cessation); the Upanishadic teachers called it the *turiya*: the fourth state; and in the Bible we find, 'Be still and know that I am God' (Psalms, 46. 10).

Advanced to one's *no-thingness*, emptied of all unwholesomeness, transcending all worldly joy, sorrow and death, the formerly turbulent stream of mortality enters into and is inseparably at-oned with the blissful ocean of immortality.

Where is the Human Race Going?

THE WORD *CONSIDER* is derived from 'con', a finite form of the Old English *cunnan* which means 'to regard studiously' or 'examine carefully', and the Latin *sidus* which means 'a star' or 'a constellation'. A star is a self-shining light. *To consider* therefore means 'to look intently at the self-shining light'. For us, this self-shining light is the constant light that shines secretly within us in the darkness of our own existential being. However, most of us are blind to this light, which is Transcendence Itself.

Why are we blind? One important reason seems to be that right from infancy we are taught that God, the magical creator of the Universe, is an Almighty Being living not in us but in some distant heaven. A child would of course find it difficult if not impossible to imagine how a being living in the sky could also be within. God is also reputed to be able to see us all and know what we are doing. He rewards goodness and punishes naughtiness. The fear of God is strong in childhood even though God's tender love for us all is taught too. To this day the devout Muslim, child or adult, will say, 'I fear God'.

As one grows up, God is presented as compassionate and merciful; he forgives those who repent. Nevertheless he is still very distant: the absolute lord and master. His light illumines the Universe; but to think of that light as also shining within you or me would generally be considered to be going a bit too far. In adulthood, man's slavery to his pleasure drive, self-indulgence and the crazy pursuit of wealth and power effectually prevents serious inquiry into the purpose(s) of existence and how to serve them.

There are those who are frankly disinterested in such inquiry. For them, God, religion and such matters are 'the business of the church and the priest'. Their own concern, they say, is with practical life.

And there are those who say, 'Show me God and the Devil in flesh and blood and I'll believe in them.'

Quite easily done. Look at yourself in a mirror. If you have clear-seeing eyes and a sound brain to interpret what you see, you will see both God and the Devil – and remember: Truth is not facetious!

So by far the greater part of the human race goes through life blind to that Transcendent Light within.

In whatever stage of development we may find ourselves, we like to know or at least to have some idea or indication of what will come next. So let us consider together. The writer, knowing that 'what he knows is that he does not know', does not presume to reveal any ultimate truth. Words like 'final', 'absolute' and 'ultimate' are troublesome words. Actually, they are tinged with relativity. If in the pursuit of Truth, each time we feel elated and say, 'At last I've got it!', we will inevitably be humbled later, if we persevere in our open-minded quest, by an even more profound discovery. In the context of the finite and temporal we can arrive at a goal, a final statement, an end-point of research, the top of Everest; but in the context of the Infinite-Eternal there is neither beginning nor ending.

So when we use the terms *Transcendence* or *God* or *Brahman* or whatever, what we are really saying is that *It* is beyond our present capacity to know, although we can *be* It. Today, largely thanks to scientific research, we know our own body fairly well. Imagine ourselves living a thousand centuries ago: how much was known in those days about the body? And yet in that era each person was the body just as much as each of us is the body today. And who can say how much has yet to be discovered about the body?

So there is no room for conceit or pride. I know that I do not know – a provisional remark, not an absolute fact. It is healthy to laugh at ourselves occasionally – not derisively but happily.

All the finest pictorial or sculptural representations of the Buddha have a gentle, enigmatic smile – like Leonardo's Mona Lisa. Could this smile be suggestive of the ineffable – and also of 'Let us get on with the job of being decent humans *now*'?

Nature evolved mammals which gave birth to live young. The mother who had carried the little one in her womb till its birth might well have felt that her progeny was part of herself. Self-love, characteristic of the animal world – and certainly of the human species – includes nurturing, sustaining, protecting, cleaning, etc. Possibly, the roots of parental love and of family feeling lie here. The whole family is the biological unit. Perhaps the Chinese were aware of this, for classically their population census used to be taken on the basis of families rather than of individuals. The break-up of the family, where the children – and sometimes the parents too – go their own separate ways, may be one of the influences leading to the rampant individualism that is prevalent today and which is so destructive of the beneficial effects of true individuality (indivisibility).

Upbringing, education and living as a member of a social group condition us all. Each and every person experiences pleasure and pain, well-being and illness; he witnesses the birth and death of relatives, friends, animals and pets. And he asks, *Where did I come from? How? Why? Where am I going – both in this life and after death?*

Let us consider the latter. We do not know anything about the after-death state with the *same kind of knowing* we enjoy in everyday life. But we do have beliefs about it, not because we have personally discovered or experienced it but because we have been conditioned to believe in our continued existence as the *same identifiable entity* that we were when alive. Since the body certainly dies and is destroyed, we believe our souls go to heaven, hell or purgatory according to the way we have lived our earthly lives. We also possess more or less detailed descriptions of these localities.

Where do animals go when they die – and how might they picture, say, heaven? Apparently, our earliest evolutionary ancestors were fish. We have five fingers because we are descended from a Devonian fish that had five phalanges or bones in its fins. In a delightfully humorous poem entitled 'Heaven', Rupert Brooke presents a fish-eye view of celestial bliss. Fish, pondering deep wisdom, say that their life in stream and pond cannot be all; somewhere beyond space and time there must be slimier slime and wetter water where swims One who is immense, squamous, omnipotent, who swam before rivers began. No angler's fly conceals a hook in the Eternal Brook; there, are heavenly weeds, and round, fat celestial caterpillars, paradisal grubs and moths and immortal flies. In their heaven, say fish, there is no land!

So too, inhabitants of some desert lands dream of fountains and couches and houris; others dream of happy hunting grounds – while probably (or is it by chance?) the mathematician in his heaven can show that $a+b$ does not $= b+a$ in all circumstances and that $qp-pq = ih/2\pi$ instead of an honest to goodness zero.

Some people believe there is no after-death state. When you die, the existential you is totally extinguished, apart from the chemical elements which composed the body. They go back into the universal stock of atoms – and the 'you' which lived continues to live only as a memory in those who knew you. Also, if you have influenced the history of your community or of all mankind, you continue to live in recorded history[1]. This 'you' which continues to live in men's memories or in recorded history is of course not the identifiable entity which was the actual living you. Every historian or biographer, being a conditioned person, unavoidably has an 'angle' and presents a picture of you which is coloured in some degree or other by his conditioning and projections. Post mortem memories and descriptions tend to resemble clouds which change shape as the wind blows. They cannot avoid

1.Old Hindu culture was singularly devoid of history in the sense in which other cultures – e.g. Greek, Islamic, European and American – have understood and recorded history. The 3rd century B.C. pillar inscriptions of the Mauryan emperor Ashoka are different, though they too contain much more moral and religious instruction than strictly descriptive history. Modern Hindu historians, however, are in line with historians the world over. Perhaps the ancient Hindu writers were inhibited by their perception of the psychological difficulties involved in strict historical writing.

adding or subtracting, extolling or denigrating in some degree or other the actual you who lived.

Then there are those who believe that your particular soul or spirit (urvan of the Zarathushtrians, jivatman of the Hindus) is immortal, a 'spark of the divine', which survives the bodily death *as a separate, permanent, identifiable entity,* and continues to live endlessly. People who hold such views do not see that the Immortal, being infinite and eternal, cannot be broken up and allocated in pieces to each separate person.

We must again stress that the whole of Transcendence, the whole of eternity and infinity, is *wholly* embodied in each person and in each and every manifestation throughout the cosmos. Any isolatively, separatively self-conscious man flowering as a fully perfected holy one sees this and is clearly conscious of it in holistic consciousness. The brain can never picture, conceive, think about or rationalize That of which you are transcendentally conscious; It is altogether unrepresentable in any sensory manner – sight, sound, touch, taste, smell – or by thought, whether abstract or discursive. In the state of Totality, of Unitary Wholeness, there is neither need nor possibility of communication. You *are* the Total Being, the One Alone.

'Looking around, the Atman Alone saw nothing other than Itself. It first said, "I am"' (Brh. Up. 1.4.1.). This 'I am' is the ahmi of Ahura Mazda, the ehiyeh of Exodus 3.14, the transcendental 'I am' which you yourself are when holistic consciousness supervenes. All distinctions, divisions, entities, particularities and separations disappear. Transcendence, the unknowable by mortality, *Is*.

'What is it?' asks child-man.

'Transcendence unknowable by mortality' is the answer; or, 'Silence'.

In Shakespeare's *The Tempest*, Ariel sings to Ferdinand:

> Full fathom five thy father lies;
> Of his bones are coral made;
> Those are pearls that were his eyes;
> Nothing of him that doth fade,
> But doth suffer a sea-change
> Into something rich and strange.

(Act 1. Sc.2. Lines 394–399)

Only a change 'into something rich and strange'! Transcendence is indeed strange, so strange that the only way to 'know' It is *to silently be It*.

I, the person who exists as a particular, finite, temporal entity, does not and cannot possess or have *an* eternal soul or spirit as if it were a separate immortal entity residing in the body. Such an impossible view was in fact held by the Empiricist philosopher John Locke, who regarded the person as a single atomic mental substance and the body, composed of many material atoms, as its property.

When a person says 'I', he is referring primarily to the living organism that bears his name. This psycho-physical organism can think, i.e. talk inaudibly; it can also feel, speak audibly and act. Action is the culmination of the process which usually originates in the psyche as desire, or the need to satisfy what is necessary for continued living, or for the expression of native talent in art, science, philosophy, mechanics, engineering, etc. All these components constituting the 'I' or 'you' are perishable. Only the Primordial Undifferentiated Creative Energy, which by self-constriction becomes the 'I' or whatever else is manifested, is immortal, infinite, eternal. All manifestation comes into finite being, exists for its temporal life-span and passes out of manifested existence. When the organism perishes, the 'I' or 'you', together with the self-consciousness which says 'I am', 'you are', become non-existent.

After death, there are no heavens, or hells. These are the absurd inventions made here-now by us who are alive. They are reflections of states of consciousness resulting from actions by both ourselves and others. By virtue of universal interactiveness and inter-relatedness, each one of us affects himself and his environment, and in certain cases the whole of mankind. For instance, a local war can flare up into a global conflagration; a new invention can find world-wide uses; the teachings of a perfected holy one may grow into a world religion; the harnessing of a newly discovered source of power like nuclear energy may prove a blessing to mankind – or blow the planet out of existence.

We, subhuman as we are, want to see those we hate or disapprove of suffer. Those whom we love and approve of we place in heaven, enjoying felicities. Examine all the descriptions of hellish tortures and heavenly felicities presented in all the religions and in the writings of Arda Viraf or Dante and other poets. They are all of the earth, earthy: projections of what subhumans have in fact done to other subhumans as well as to some true humans (the martyred saints). And it is believed that the immortal and hence immaterial soul suffers or enjoys the consequences of the material organism's misdeeds or good deeds! How can this possibly happen? How can a finite mortal produce an infinite consequence?

Furthermore, all these subhuman absurdities are ascribed to God's Divine Justice! Aristotle probably gave one of the best conceptions of justice in his *Nicomachean Ethics*, Book 5, Chapter 2. Briefly stated, justice is the *practice of perfect virtue to others and also to oneself*. Surely justice should act as a healing power, neither retributive nor rewarding. Punishment is a confession of our failure to love, educate and heal. Holding out the carrot of earthly or heavenly delights is sheer bribery – and unpersuasive, as history shows.

Consider a very simple matter. Religions declare that God is omnipresent. Quite true, for Transcendence is omnipresent. But how many in the world have lived or live as if they were well aware of that omnipresence? Of the few who are aware, how many live virtuously out of fear? How many out of love? And wisdom? Consider also another matter. Jesus gave his life as a ransom for the many. He did it as a vicarious atonement for our sins – and only a sinless one can do that – and to save our souls. The perpetrators of the Inquisition burnt thousands at the stake for their heresies – entirely forgetting that all authentic spiritual teachers were branded 'heretics' in some way or other – also to save their souls! But surely if they had been faithfully following the example of Jesus they would have immolated themselves in their autodafés. Perhaps inquisitors do not like great heat! They have many confrères in non-religious fields.

Proponents of the Indian doctrine of karma (and its accompanying doctrine of rebirth) believe that it represents the full working out of perfect justice. It recognizes that every thought, feeling, word and deed is a causal energy actively effecting a change: its vipaka or result. I myself generated in my past lives and keep generating in my present life all the causes, mental and material, good and evil, constructive and destructive, of which I will experience the due effects in this or future lives.

Theoretically it may sound fair. In the popular mind, it works in a tit-for-tat fashion: you helped me out of difficulty in the past, so now I help you; or you lent me £10, so now I return you £10 – with or without interest?! But in actual life such mechanical exactitude does not hold good. Our own living process and the whole environmental or world living process are both far too complex for any such simplistic exactitude. The writer knows of an otherwise intelligent person who saw in the Hiroshima horror the perfect working out of the Law of Karma. It was the karma of just those hundred thousand men, women, children and babies to be there in Hiroshima when the bomb was dropped. It was the Vipaka they reaped for the negative karma sown in the past; it was 'their karma' to be atomized! Could anything be more absurd, inhuman or impossible?

The Law of Karma is valid – but intelligent believers sometimes fail to understand how it really works. We know for certain that every force in action leads to a consequence unless a counteracting force annuls it or changes the degree, direction and nature of the effect. Karma functions in a particular and also in a general way. Drink too much alcohol every day and you *will* quite possibly develop cirrhosis of the liver. Thoughts can have a more widespread and destructive effect. The thoughts of Fichte, Hegel, Nietzsche, Wagner – 'Herrenvolk', 'Master Morality', the 'Great Ego', etc. – climaxed in six million Jews being murdered during Hitler's short-lived domination of Germany. If the Mosaic Law – a life for a life – be applied karmically, how will the appropriate consequences be wreaked upon the few thousand who caused the Holocaust?

And there is also this to consider. Since each one of us is all humanity, how does karma work out for us? We must never forget that each of us is responsible for all, each one of us is his brother's keeper – a fact, not merely a pious sentiment.

If we are intelligent we shall see that there is no option for us but to practise perfect virtue towards all and also towards ourselves. This means universal brotherhood, which requires universal love. But if you do not have wisdom you cannot love. And if you do not have love, even the modicum with which Nature endowed you, you do not seek wisdom.

Reject all philosophies and teachings whose main roots are not love and wisdom. If love and wisdom are your roots, only then will the Tree of Life in Eden bear truly *human* blossoms – as indeed it was intended to do. Not man but Transcendence Alone is Superman.

So do not cling to the idea of karma as if it were Newton's Third Law: action and reaction are equal and opposite. Or as if it were Schopenhauer's Theory of Palingenesis: the continual rebirth, not of an individual life after life, but of the blind will to live – the Buddhist tanha – considered as a metaphysical entity.

As to rebirth, the only transmigrant is the Transcendent: God in Totality producing, maintaining and transforming (through death) the multiplicity of that Totality. And do not cling to the 'I', which is illusory: an ever-appearing and disappearing maya. Karma, like divine justice, is a healing power, neither retributive nor rewarding. It is an equilibrative power, more akin to counterpoint in music than the ponderously exact balancing of the dishes of a pair of scales.

The dualistic subhuman thinks in terms of retributive punishments and gratuitous rewards, and lives accordingly. The holy one, a creator, only creates, even as Transcendence creates, and, like Transcendence, is free of dualistic consequence. Any man who lives virtuously discovers that virtue is its own reward. If he desires a reward for being virtuous, that virtue is tainted. Health, wholeness, holiness are all one and the same.

Righteous living is the natural expression of your own rightness. Cultivated righteousness will fail you under sufficiently provocative circumstances, especially if your self-esteem is likely to be dented or some deep-seated desire thwarted.

How do I discover what is right?

Remember that destructiveness or hatred spring from frustrated greed. Carefully observe what harms your neighbour and yourself too. If you hate yourself, you are well set for hating and hurting others – and here 'others' includes the entire sentient world. Watch all your fantasies very carefully, for all one's imaginings charge the psychical atmosphere with good or evil influences. Living the pure human life is indeed a very difficult task. I must never think that no one is looking at my secret thoughts and feelings. *I myself am looking without knowing that I am looking. I myself am the Lord of Karma, the dispenser of justice.* This is a fact all too little understood or taken into account at the subhuman stage.

We human beings are so made up that the inmost deep of our consciousness – wrongly called the unconscious – where God resides or Shiva 'touches' us, knows and sees everything, creates situations and draws everything that happens in our lives towards us. Man, superficially free to 'do what he likes', can, unless prevented by some external force stronger than himself, or by his conscience, certainly do so. But he has no power over consequence, for Transcendence within him sees to that. That is why in the previous paragraph it was stated that the Lord of Karma is oneself. Unfortunately, neither parent nor teacher nor priest is awake to this. In consequence, man, having over-procreated himself, languishes like a forsaken orphan when it comes to the most important thing in his life: his spiritual nurture.

This inmost deep of consciousness comes fully awake in Buddhahood and Christhood. Then child-man has blossomed into the omniscience of the perfected holy one. He is the virtuous one.

In the *Bhagavad Gita* (16.2.), detailing the virtues characterizing the person who is a true human, Shri Krishna begins significantly with ahimsa, harmlessness, and then adds truthfulness, mildness, freedom from anger, non-grasping, compassion to all living, modesty, freedom from fault-finding, vigour, forgiveness, fortitude, purity and finally absence of pride and malice.

It is wise to reflect deeply upon the different ways in which virtue is presented in Buddhist teaching and in other religions. The Buddha had compassionate understanding for all that lives. His superb psychological insight showed him clearly that mankind did not know the meaning of virtue, for, as Plato pointed out several decades later, a man really knows only what he can actually do. By and large man's life then as in our own day, was not exactly virtuous – and the Buddha knew that a man will react strongly against anyone who baldly tells him the truth, at the same time chiding him to mend his ways. Self-pride and self-conceit require delicate, skilful handling!

So the Buddha did not lay down commandments of the kind that occur in most religions. Instead, he presented a code of behaviour in the form of five moral advices (Pancha Sila) for monk, nun and layman alike. He advised them (note the negative formulation) to refrain from: (1) injuring living beings, (2) taking anything which is not given, (3) sensual (especially sexual) indulgence, (4) false or injurious speech, and (5) alcoholic liquors and other substances that befuddle consciousness. For ordained monks and nuns there are many additional rules.

Restraint of greed, hatred, all impulses to vice and disharmonious action prepares the ground in the psyche for the seeds of virtue to grow. Order, health and peace will then quite organically emerge out of disorder and dis-ease.

This is not a fanciful utopian dream but life in fullness.

•

Let us now consider the present global situation.

Elephantiasis (or Titanism) seems to be the prevailing disease. Since the last world war everything has expanded or inflated out of all proportion: crime (especially violent crime), nuclear and other weapons of mass destruction, pollution, fear and suspicion between nations, terrorism, strikes, corruption, packaged entertainment (deprived of spontaneity can there be true happiness?), prices and wages, advertising, the production of consumer goods (with built-in obsolescence), institutions and business organizations, etc., etc. We have our giant multi-national corporations, supertankers and supermarkets, jumbo jets and mega-stores. At the same time it has become fashionable to regard words like 'virtue', 'purity', 'modesty', 'morality', etc., as off-putting or 'square'.

The source of evil lies within ourselves. If I look carefully within myself I see that fundamentally it is *my* greed that causes inflation. *My* self-conceit exalts me above my neighbour; so I compete with him and try to defeat him to prove my superiority. It is *my* hate, fear and suspicion that lead to wars, oppression and exploitation;

my insensitivity to the well-being of the underprivileged which contributes to or even brings about their miserable condition.

It may be argued that the Welfare State takes care of all this. Yes, it alleviates up to a point; but socialized concern is merely the measure of the failure of human love. Insofar as I care genuinely and freely give what I can give, I am human; if human love and giving fail, however, other agencies must fill the gap. Thus I discover that at the sub-human stage I am both godly and devilish, and the rest of the species *homo* is the same.

Homo sapiens – and we may add *et amans*, for wisdom and love go together – is therefore a state towards which we are developing – rather slowly . . .

We have amassed technical knowledge and skills to an amazing degree, but have lagged sadly behind in terms of moral and spiritual development. Goaded by the pleasure-drive, enslaved by self-indulgence, dismally ignorant of the purpose(s) of existence, deficient in self-knowledge, we move inexorably towards the brink of doom. Despite the occasional treaty partially halting the proliferation of nuclear weaponry, technological man has it in his power to exterminate the living world. If he makes a mistake, even a slight mistake, it could spell the end of life on Earth, perhaps the end of the planet itself.

Man makes good resolves and signs hopeful treaties, influenced by fear of destruction. Unfortunately, fear never brings *lasting* good results. Throughout history the state of the world has always reflected just what we ourselves are. Beliefs, plans, systems, blueprints, programmes, methods and all thought-out procedures emanating from unholistic consciousness are ultimately incapable of bringing in-depth change for good. Only a radical transformation of consciousness can avert our nemesis. It has therefore become an acute necessity. Consequently, it is the responsibility of each person in the world to open himself to that transformation, for it is the psychological factor – the mode in which we are aware of our selves, of the world, and of the relationship maintaining between each of us and the whole world – which bears most upon the fate of our species and of the small but beautifully balanced planet that it inhabits.

•

William Sharp, the Pre-Raphaelite poet who used the pseudonym Fiona Macleod, wrote:

> I dreamed of Orchil, the dim goddess who is under the brown earth
> in a vast cavern, where she weaves at two looms.
> With one hand she weaves Life upward through the grass;
> With the other she weaves Death downward through the mould.
>
> And the sound of the weaving is Eternity,
> And the name of it in the green world is Time,
> And through all, Orchil weaves the weft of Eternal Beauty,
> Eternal beauty that passeth not though its soul is Change.

The voice of the poet, like the voice of the mystic and the fully-fledged human, sings of eternity. He could sing equally well of infinity and immortality, for this triad is of the very substance and nature of Transcendence, as well as the context in which the Primordial Creative Energy functions and acts.

William Sharp wrote of Orchil weaving Life and Death. I would rather say birth and death, for Life, in its transcendent reality, is eternal. It is our organic life which manifests itself between the complementary poles of birth and death. In our subhuman state we can be conscious only in terms of the complementary poles and of the in-between shadow-play projected by Eternal Life on the screen of matter. We have only evolved to the extent that we are able to see the shadow-play (manifestation) and mistake it for the Whole Reality; we experience the illusion and believe it to be the Truth.

Long ago in India they called this shadow-play *maya*. So today. And tomorrow? Bear in mind that the whole of what we subhumans call the past, the present and the future is cradled simultaneously in eternity, so the Transcendent Holy One is omniscient, all-seeing and all knowing.

How may you or I glimpse tomorrow?

The answer is simple: *Look intently at what is here*. Look within. Look now. But look as silently as possible, free of the brain's constant chatter. Look with love free of desire for personal gain; with love that is at peace. Look intelligently – that is, selflessly and dispassionately. Intelligence is the faculty to see the truth of things without bias or prejudice or rigid belief. Wisdom is that action which is the outcome of intelligence and love. Looking intelligently is like God looking at creation through your eyes.

Man is fundamentally a religious being; only secondarily, very secondarily, is he a political, economic, social and gregarious creature. What does the word 'religion' mean? Cicero (B.C. 106–43) derived *religio* from *relegere*, 'to gather together'. In the *Ahuramazda Yasht* of the Zarathushtrians, Zarathushtra asks God his names. Ahura-Mazda lists twenty names of which the second is *the Gatherer*, the Divine Shepherd. The first name is *ahmi*, 'I Am' and the twentieth is *Ahmi yat ahmi*, 'I Am That I Am'. In Exodus, 3.14, we have Moses being instructed by JHWH-ELOHIM, the Lord God, speaking out of the burning bush, to say to the Israelites *Ehiyeh asher ehiyeh*, 'I Am That I Am'. The root of the Hebrew *Ehiyeh* is the same as that of *JHWH*. For thousands of years, the holistically conscious prophets or mystics have been regarded as identical with Transcendence, as the Supreme Being.

Servius and Lactantius (known as the Christian Cicero of the 3rd century A.D.), and later still St. Augustine (354–430 A.D.), Bishop of Hippo, in his *Retractiones* (1.13), derived *religio* from *religare* (root *lig*, 'to bind') which means, 'to bind back' [to God, the Origin]. This is in line with the Sanskrit *yuj*, the root of *yoga*, meaning 'to restore man to his Source'.

When we first sense, even dimly, that we are not the pinnacle of creation but that there is *That* which transcends us, our hitherto dormant religious sense has begun to stir. If it grows, we feel we owe obedience and reverence to that which transcends us. Obedience (from *ob* and *audire*, 'to hear') essentially means 'to listen to', 'to give ear to'. If this feeling is nurtured with care and love, and if intellectual perception intensifies it, we feel willing and ready to worship the Transcendent – that is, to hold it as supremely worthy. In culmination, we long to be united with It and be at home in It throughout our life.

Inflexibly materialistic scientists tend to scorn all this. Nevertheless there have been and still are scientists who are religious and have testified sincerely and sensibly to Transcendence – scientists of the calibre of Einstein, Max Planck, De Broglie, Schroedinger, Jeans, Eddington, Bohm and several others. And it may well turn out that the work of modern scientists will be one of the powerful promoters of the religious vision of life and of religious (i.e. truly human) living.

Science is the investigation of the concrete manifestation of the Primordial Undifferentiated Creative Energy. Religion is the discovery of the laws whose working out or expression is the Mind aspect of the Creative Power. Religion includes ethics, virtue, and thus is indispensible for truly human fulfilment. The discovery of laws puts power into man's hands; the constructive and right use of that power depends upon virtue and spiritual intelligence; that is, upon unerring insight (buddhi, nous). Consider what has been done by man and what has happened to man from the day of his discovery of stone implements and the bow-and-arrow to the day of $E=mc^2$. Please *do* consider or we shall lose our divine right to belong to the species *homo sapiens*.

We may see then that whatsoever purifies, heals and perfects a man, relates him rightly and fully to life, and enables him to realize Transcendence in clear consciousness and live by that realization, is religion.

Whoever is moved to respond sympathetically to this may be impelled to ask, 'Who will teach me? What is the way?' Truly, the best answer out of several possible answers, is, surprisingly enough, 'You will teach yourself!' One incomparable teacher affirmed, 'Look within – you are Buddha'. Another affirmed, 'I am the Way, the Truth, the Life'. Say that to yourself if you mean business – again and again.

Your own living body, the psycho-physical organism, provides the way. Study it carefully both physiologically and psychologically, and discover what you are actually. Learn how the body is constituted, how it works, and what its true needs are, not its false appetites. This will also tell you a good deal about your own psychological aspect.

Watch your thoughts and feelings. Question them, challenge them, probe deeply and understand them. Thus you will come to love yourself without false self-approbation. After all, you alone know best the secret workings of your brain and heart. Free of self-deprecation, possessed of pure self-love, you can love everyone else, for everyone else in the world is, like you, like me, a mixed dish of devilishness and godliness.

The Buddha declared: 'He who lives without hurting others, lives with a self become Brahman (Transcendence)'. What a wonderful insight – and with such profound and wide consequences! He also taught us to eschew self-indulgence, which makes it possible for us to make right, healthy and profitable use, both physically and spiritually, of all our senses and any faculties with which we are gifted. Let all observation and study be open-minded. Inquire seriously and be free of bias, prejudice, preconception and assumption.

When you really know yourself through constant inquiry and dispassionate observation, you will easily understand the ways of most men, for each and every one of us is a variation played by eternal life on the theme of man. You and I are therefore just different versions of each other. If each person skilfully plays the melody of his own life, joyously and lovingly, we will all together make a grand harmony: humanity's music.

Learn, then, from your own body; treat it as your guru. Learn too from all other bodies. The living person is the way. Innermost consciousness, which is also divine consciousness, the universal consciousness of the One Total Reality, is the traveller on the way. Being universal, whatever you realize of truth, goodness and beauty affects the consciousness of all mankind.

Like universal space, consciousness takes in everything and affects everything as it gives room to everything to exist, to move about and grow. 'Quod superius sicut quod inferius': 'As above, so below.' It is easy to use this ancient teaching mistakenly, however, as when we project above what maintains below. Man is accustomed to the idea of a national or group leader, with ministers and officers ranging down in a hierarchical stratum to the humblest workers. Correspondingly, there are God, archangels, angels and the entire heavenly pantheon down to innumerable minor spirits performing their small appointed functions. And there are heavenly rewards and hellish punishments as in our mortal sphere, for man generally has not seen that the transcendent context of the Infinite-Eternal negates all finite-temporal systems, conceptions and methods. The perfected one in holistic consciousness is in fact God on earth manifest as perfect humanity. When God on earth relinquishes his divine manifestation, the mortal's awareness of Transcendence is like the light of the moon, for that light has undergone a diminishment of its sun-like radiance.

As pointed out earlier, the split in consciousness between self and not-self is a root-source of the world's evil and sorrow. One of the world's oldest, humane and sensible teachings is, 'Love your neighbour as yourself' (Lev. 19. 18.). Who is my neighbour? What is my neighbour? The very next person to me, someone on the other side of the world, you who read this, the sinner, the saint, the callous murderer, the innocent kidnap victim and also the kidnapper himself – all are my neighbours. Every animal, every tree, every blade of grass, even the thorn on the stem of the rose, is my neighbour.

The devil is one of my near neighbours. In fact he makes himself at home inside me! And, as the Muslims say, God is 'closer to me than my jugular vein!' Shall I pick and choose whom or what I shall love? I am no true lover if I do! Or shall I *be love?* Then indeed Transcendence will put me into the heart of the Infinite-Eternal! And the tears of the world will be transmuted into Fountains of Divine Compassion.

This is not mere poetic effusion. It is living truth . . . But do not *believe* a word I say; rather, consider it and become the living truth yourself – and then you will enjoy the sweet nectar of immortality wherever you are. No need then to go to paradise; *now-here* is your salvation and the world's salvation.

•

Religions have taught that God is omnipresent. How many of the 5,000,000,000 people existing today live as if God were indeed omnipresent – looking at you – pleading with you to come home?

Transcendence the Infinite-Eternal is indeed omnipresent, unavoidably so, and in timeless conjunction with Its created Totality. Has that wonderful, sublime and terrible affirmation, 'Aham brahma'smi', 'I and the Father are One', ever pierced your heart, rushed through your blood like a fiery baptismal stream and transmuted your isolative, separative, God-and-Truth-denying consciousness into holistic consciousness, which like the consciousness of God is all-inclusive, rejecting nothing, not even Satan and satanic Evil, because Its transcendent love and wisdom know that nothing can be cast out of Its own created Universe, that everything can be, has to be and will be transformed, redeemed, and gathered into its everlasting embrace?

But what especially has evolution done in and for the living world?

We discern growing and expanding grades of consciousness throughout the living order and in man their potential culmination in experience of and union with the Origin. The whole evolutionary and developmental process therefore invites and inspires man towards the realization of holistic consciousness. This is the answer to the question, 'Where is the human race going?' It is Orchil weaving Life upward through the grass.

Today we know that the mortal psycho-physical organism regarded by itself is an organic whole. Many people, through conditioning, believe there is a spiritual component in them. Healed of all ill, there are those who know in clear consciousness that Transcendence completely permeates them. Taking into account the immaterial, immortal constituent which most people accept on faith, we may well say that a full description of man would be that he is a spiritual and organic whole, because, during the last few millennia, the fair and patient planet Earth has been blessed by the presence of perfected holy ones, such as the founders of the great religions as well as scores of other authentic spiritual teachers. These are the 'sons of God', Brahmaputras, the embodiments of transcendent virtues such as Love, Wisdom Truth, Goodness, Grace and Beauty. They possessed perfect poise and equanimity. They obeyed the directives of the Supreme. Equipped with unequalled understanding of human nature, they were the healers of mankind. They were true *humans*.

Never say, 'All that is quite beyond me'. If you say so you deny your human potency, your blissful creativeness.

In his poem, 'Adonais' (lines 460–466), Shelley wrote:

> The One remains, the many change and pass;
> Heaven's light forever shines, Earth's shadows fly;
> Life, like a dome of many-coloured glass
> Stains the white radiance of Eternity,
> Until Death tramples it to fragments. – Die,
> If thou wouldst be with that which thou dost seek!
> Follow where all is fled!

'Die, if thou wouldst be with that which thou dost seek' – that is, die to all worldliness if it is Transcendence you seek. Seek rightly, therefore, and all that is needed for the seeking will be given you. 'Follow where all is fled' – that is, fearlessly enter the empty void, the creative source of the plenitude.

Lines 478–486 in the same poem assure us:

> That Light whose smile kindles the Universe,
> That Beauty in which all things work and move,
> That Benediction which the eclipsing Curse
> Of Birth can quench not, that sustaining Love
> Which through the web of being blindly wove
> By man and beast and earth and air and sea,
> Burns bright or dim, as each are mirrors of
> The fire for which all thirst; now beams on me,
> Consuming the last clouds of cold mortality.

The temporal life and death of the human organism is the phantom play of Eternal Life whose eternal beauty does not pass though its soul be *change* – change being the changeless fact of all manifestation. So stars and planets; men, women and gods – all manifest and pass away into the Infinite-Eternal. Having dropped every vestige of shape and form, stripped of all isolation, they return home, transmuted into the Primordial Undifferentiated Creative Energy of Transcendence, in which death holds no sway.

But what is this death that afflicts all manifestation,

that causes us fear and grief? It is change so great, so total a dissolution of organic existence,[1] So beyond all of man's perception, that our passionate but foolish clinging to endless, separate egoity is completely extinguished. But that which is beyond our knowledge, beyond our most penetrating perceptions, is Transcendence Itself, the Deathless. At present we are incapable of being holistically conscious, so we weep when death opens the door to supreme bliss and peace. We have forgotten that we are divinity confined and so we are blind to the light of living truth.

Therefore, consider carefully, consider peacefully, and see and know that we humans are the harbingers of eternity. For who else on Earth but we can sing the Song of Eternal Life through all of ever-dying time? Who else on Earth can unveil the beautiful face of the Infinite as we dance our way through the measureless expanses of space?

To this indeed is man going: to the infinity and eternity of Transcendence in holistic consciousness – to the love and wisdom, the truth and beauty of Transcendence.

When will he arrive?

Never in time, but certainly *here-now* in the immediacy of the eternal living present moment.

How will he do it?

By living the religious life, which is none other than the whole of the secular life lived virtuously.

Wholly beyond, unseizable and simultaneously at one with all – this is the Truth: silent, still, alone . . .

Be well and happy; and good speed along your own unique way.

[1]Remember that literally 'existence' is 'a standing out of the blissful Infinite-Eternal'.

Epilogue – Peace

THE YOUNG BOY who asked, 'What is immortality?', pursued that question for several decades until at last he saw that the answer was ineffable: that it was meaningful solely in terms of transformed being. Nevertheless, a few suggestions may be offered for consideration here.

All of us who are not yet fully-fledged humans are conscious of the entire world process in terms of uprising-proceeding-ending; in other words, of birth-life-death. Ending is a certainty for whatever begins, death for any creature that is born.

In actual fact, what we see is constant change, but since we are still conscious solely in the mode of mortality, we see death as the lord of all existence.

Insofar as change is the mark of all manifestation, what we really have is a continuous series of changed states. This is, however, only the verbal expression of an intellectual perception. But if our mental perception blossoms into full consciousness, death or ending as we see or feel it now will give place to a conscious awareness of the permanency of mutable manifestation, which implies that Transcendence and existence are one – immortal.

In that consciousness which functions in the mode of immortality, there are no breaks; that is, no deaths or endings, and therefore no births or beginnings. Duality no longer imprisons us, nor unidirectional continuity (time). There is only Totality and simultaneity and immediacy (eternity). Static and dynamic have no meaning in eternity and infinity. Also, there is no duality of active-passive, no God *and* Universe (Nature). Creation alone is here: total and immeasurable God-Being: the Unitary Whole.

Breathe easily until the duality of in-breath and out-breath is integrated and transcended into the unitary wholeness of *Breathing*, of Living, and you will know in full that Brahman (Transcendence, God) is prana or life-breath (C.U.4.10.4): breath not merely as a mixture of nitrogen and oxygen but as pneuma (Πνευμα , spirit).

•

Our daily life is a constant stream of overlapping thoughts and feelings, words and actions. We associate the self with each and every one of these – *I thought, I felt, I said, I did,* etc. The brain talks ceaselessly as it registers and reacts to this stream. This chatter signifies that consciousness is functioning in the mode of mortality.

Holistic consciousness functions in the mode of immortality. It is clearly aware that ending or death is not annihilation. Death is a change of a familiar form into something so different that ordinary consciousness cannot perceive the relationship between the new and the old, though holistic consciousness can.

Avoiding the error of attempting to *achieve* or *attain* holistic consciousness, we can live in such manner as to enable holistic consciousness to supervene. As suggested in Chapter 7, use each and every sense faculty fully, paying complete attention *without reacting* for or against whatever you observe no matter what its quality. This has to be a constant practice throughout the day. Our conflicts, miseries and inward disturbances mostly arise reactively when what we observe clashes with our desires and predilections. In addition, living a righteous daily life – righteous as you yourself understand it – is indispensable.

Regarding reactive observation, suppose for example I see an impatient mother smacking her baby for wetting itself, or an irate father clouting his son for displeasing him, my unprintable reactions in thought and feeling only increase the stresses of the situation. Why heap Pelion upon Ossa? My reactions release harmful chemicals in my body, make it easier for me to repeat my folly and are of no help to the young victim in either case. But if I remain quiet within myself, I might well be able to make the right response, if circumstances allow it; if not, a kindly look may be sufficient. There is so much horror in the world which we *have* to endure in silence simply because we cannot do anything about it.

Now it is difficult *not* to react – and react strongly – to much that we observe. But with perseverance and dispassion it is possible to observe everything without reaction. Then, the psyche being calm, we can change what is bad into good, and what is good into better. Also, the inconsequential chatter of the brain diminishes and eventually ceases when all sense-functioning is pacified (*pacified*, NOT *repressed*). You are then in a state of silence, equanimity and poise. This state is not passivity nor mere quietism or 'holy indifference'; and you are decidedly not unconscious. You are in fact transcendentally awake, conscious of Creative Action in Eternity, for you as the isolatively self-conscious entity obstructing the light of Transcendence are no more. You have died to the 'you' and are changed into the You through whom Transcendence realizes Its own transcendence as the perfect human. Then you the self and all that is outside your skin, the not-self, are one living harmony; and you see quite clearly that what we ordinarily call death is not annihilation but so great a change from the familiar to the unfamiliar that ordinary consciousness cannot comprehend it, though holistic consciousness can.

In the ordinary way, the succession of sense impressions, actions and experiences gives rise to breaks in your consciousness. You are 'born' when an impression or experience with which you associate yourself begins, and you 'die' when it ends. This is the factual meaning of reincarnation: the succession of 'lives' during the single lifetime of the apparent organism from 'birth' to 'death'.

When, by living the truly religious life – which is no other than the whole of the secular life lived as a sacrificial gift of your whole self to Transcendence in unconditional love – you are blessed by the vision of the Truth, you 'know' Transcendence by being one with it. Unobstructive to essential wholeness, utterly silent and still, you are conscious in the mode of immortality, choicelessly 'knowing' and 'being' the Immortal.

Temporal life is the gracious gift by Transcendence, mediated through Nature, to us. It is our opportunity to experience the nature of immortality whilst we live. It is our hall of learning; and mortality, through the lesson of birth and death, is our teacher. Eternal life is the prerogative of Transcendence. Immortality is the silence. In the still silence is peace. The peace of Transcendence is reflected in manifestation by the immensity of the peace of the solitude between the stars.

All worldly living is restlessness. With true vision, the turbulent motion from birth to death ceases; sorrow, confusion and ignorance have ended; vibrant quiescence prevails. It is the peace of God passing all mortal understanding. The vision, the experience and actually being Transcendence is the Infinite-Eternal, the One Unitary Whole, the One Without a Second. I – not the 'I-am-I' of organic selfness but the selfless 'I' of holistic consciousness – affirm that this Infinite-Eternal is the transmutation of birth-death into peaceful, eternal Being. For you, for me, the silence is the supreme freedom, the perfect peace.

Silent and still, 'unmoving' yet everywhere and *now-here*, 'inactive' yet ceaselessly creating in conjunction with the Creative Power, you have transcended existence. No more a *standing out* of Transcendence, you are a truly human being. Done is what had to be done; you are now not only *at peace* but you *are peace* itself, radiant peace. From now on you can be conscious in the mode of immortality, as and when you please, whilst still living in the body.

The continuity of the birth-death world process is, to your consciousness, a non-continuous wholeness, silent and still, here-now. The discontinuous energy-pulsation of the immanent birth-death world process[1] is to your consciousnes the Immutable Actuality, the Eternal Truth, silent and still. You *have* to be silent and still to be superconsciously aware of all this, because Transcendence is silent and still and can only be so in the context of infinity and eternity.

Whilst functioning in holistic consciousness, no awareness of separate selfhood is possible. Holistic consciousness is not yours, not mine. It is the One Unitary Consciousness of the One Unitary Whole.

In the transcendent conjugation of Divine Love, all separate selfhood, be it of God as postulated by man or of man who is received into the transcendent action

[1]Transcendentally it is the life/new life world process.

of Divine Love, has vanished. There is only the Divine Loving, only the Divine Action of Divine Love.

For manifestation to be, the One becomes the two, the three, the countless many – all existence. For fulfilment, all existence contracts into less than the many: into the three, the two, the One – and the One becomes the No-thing, the Unknowable, but into That which you, I, the countless many and all existence will be absorbed.

This is not to the taste of the many today. They want their little insignificant selves to remain separate, the source of sorrow and defeat for themselves and for all other small fry dragged into their nets. St. Paul declared (Romans 6.23) that 'The wages of sin is death', sin being whatever spoils or dents the unity of the Universe.

Do not ask questions about all this in the worldly mode, for all such questions cannot by their nature apply in the immortal context of the Infinite-Eternal. Just *look* and keep looking, with the psyche *calm and empty*, and your destiny will work itself out. Those who 'think' about immortality are wasting their time. Childhood is the time for questions. Then you are allowed a play-time spun out of the immeasurable plenitude of eternity. As a grown up man or woman, fully engaged with all that is grave and constant in human life, plunge into the Transcendent Void.

Consider deeply the significance of Gabriel's command to Muhammad: *'Recite!'* Gabriel did not say, *'Think!'*. Moses prevaricated with JHWH-ELOHIM that he was not eloquent, and the Lord God offered him the help of the strong tongue of his elder brother Aaron (the name means 'Enlightened [or Illumined] One'). So Moses fulfilled the divine mandate; Muhammad repeated what Gabriel recited, and the Quran was born.

When the brain stops talking – naturally and not by using drugs or practising psychic circus tricks – discursive thinking fades away. You then bid farewell to worldly consciousness and mortality. Transcendentally conscious *now-here* in the mode of immortality, there is no more uprising-proceeding-ending, no more birth-death. You are *living*, not just existing, in the context of infinity and eternity. Time, fully integrated into eternity, stands still; space as a separating gap is absorbed into infinity. Space-time is the unitarily whole abode of manifestation.

The state of the world faithfully reflects our own state

– your state, my state, everyone's state. The mothers and fathers of the world, the teachers, companions and friends, and those who govern nations and states and are responsible for law and order, hold the keys of heaven in their hands. Let no person shirk his responsibility. It is the folly and weakness of mankind to look to an external Messiah instead of being the Messiah to oneself. Resurrection and ascension have to be preceded by crucifixion, not of the flesh in our day and age but of worldliness and the insane pursuit of pleasure, wealth and power. Live virtuously and all that is needful will come to you; fail to do so and not only will you not know the serenity, bliss and fulfilment that come from having properly discharged the purposes of existence but there will in all likelihood be much suffering and confusion as well.

So the good way, the right way, is the truly happy way. Happiness and goodness always go together. And peace will be yours. The great sages of India pronounced their blessing after teaching: 'Aum shantih [peace], shantih, shantih.' The bequest of Jesus to his disciples was, 'Peace I leave with you. My peace I give unto you, not as the world giveth give I unto you' (John, 14.27). So shall you establish peace and be a blessing to mankind and all the world.

How many of the more than 5,000 million people in the world today respond to Transcendence embodied within them? Transcendence will never fail to answer in the right way if only you will call.

In one of the daily prayers of the Zarathushtrians the 'Jasa me avanghahey Mazda' ('Come to my aid, O Lord of Wisdom'), there are these words: 'I esteem the good religion of the Wisdom-worshippers, which puts an end to quarrels and causes one to put away offensive weapons.' Prior to those words are affirmations of praise for good thought, good word and good deed. We see, then, that harmful thought, word or deed is an offensive weapon, not conducive to peace either within ourselves or in our relationships with our whole environment.

Wisely, then, watch every thought, word and deed; observe exactly what you are; discover your uniqueness; awaken to the hidden light within you. Live by that light. Initially there will be tribulation, for you may at first not see beauty in the mirror of truth; but persevere living by *your* light and looking with that dispassionate love which the Buddhists call upekkha. Slowly, the beast will change. For you and I, who are beast by descent – we all have something of the reptile in us – will surely become beauty; not the beauty of our desires or projections but the beauty of our own unique human-ness. And when you see this there will be deep content and peace, and joy such as millions never know. Wherever you are and whatever you are, duke or dustman, housewife or heroine, you will be essentially right, fulfilling your own particular destiny, wanted and indispensable to life just there and just that.

Don't think, 'How can I, an insignificant nobody in the midst of 5,000 millions, make any difference in the world?'

Don't worry about the world. That is the business of Transcendence. Your business is to be your own true self.

One shining sun gives light and life to the world. One pulsing star gives joy to all who look and guidance to the traveller. You are not different from that star, that sun.

You are the immortally beloved of Transcendence.

Index